CAPTIVE STATE

LOUISIANA *and the* MAKING *of* MASS INCARCERATION

ERIC SEIFERTH,
KEVIN T. HARRELL,
KATHERINE JOLLIFF DUNN
curators

NICK WELDON
editor

THE HISTORIC
NEW ORLEANS COLLECTION
2025

THE HISTORIC NEW ORLEANS COLLECTION *(HNOC) is dedicated to the stewardship of the history and culture of New Orleans and the Gulf South. The HNOC is operated by the Kemper and Leila Williams Foundation, a Louisiana nonprofit corporation.*

533 Royal Street
New Orleans, LA 70130
www.hnoc.org

Editor: Nick Weldon
Director of publications: Jessica Dorman
President and CEO: Daniel Hammer
Design: Benjamen Purvis

First edition.

Printed in Minnesota by Point B Solutions.

29 28 27 26 25 1 2 3 4 5
ISBN: 978-0-917860-94-2

Library of Congress Cataloging-in-Publication Data
Names: Seiferth, Eric curator | Harrell, Kevin T. curator | Dunn, Katherine Jolliff curator | Weldon, Nick, 1987- editor | Historic New Orleans Collection host institution
Title: Captive state : Louisiana and the making of mass incarceration / Eric Seiferth, Kevin T. Harrell, PhD, and Katherine Jolliff Dunn, curators ; Nick Weldon, editor.
Other titles: Captive state (2025)
Description: First edition. | New Orleans, LA : The Historic New Orleans Collection, 2025. | Based on the exhibition "Captive State" which was held at the Historic New Orleans Collection from July 2024 to February 2025. | Includes bibliographical references.
Identifiers: LCCN 2025003903 | ISBN 9780917860942 paperback
Subjects: LCSH: Mass incarceration--Louisiana--History--Exhibitions | Prisoners--Louisiana--History--Exhibitions | Racism against Black people--Louisiana--Exhibitions | Louisiana--History--Exhibitions | LCGFT: Exhibition catalogs
Classification: LCC HV9475.L2 C34 2025 | DDC 365/.609763--dc23/eng/20250515
LC record available at https://lccn.loc.gov/2025003903

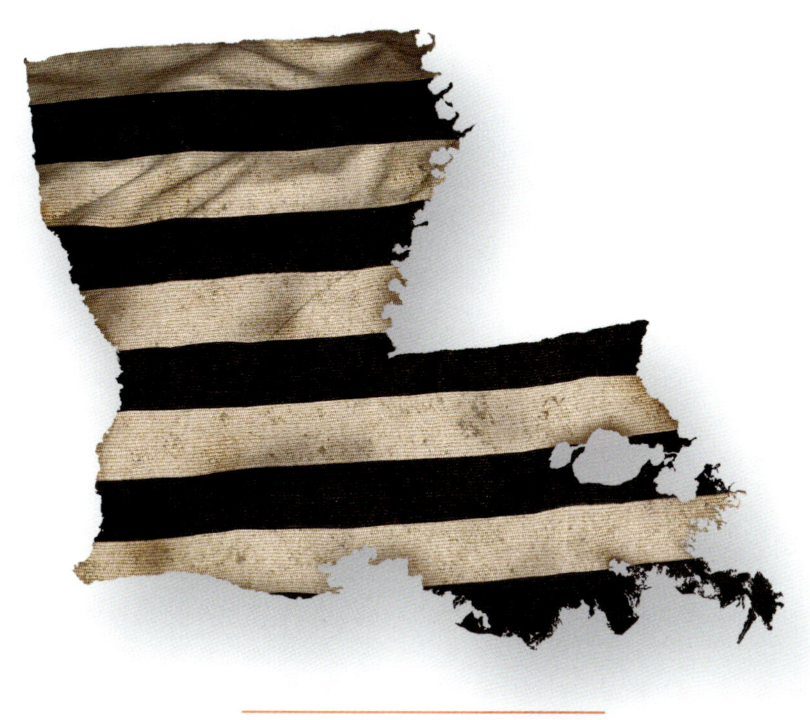

The institutions of **SLAVERY** *and* **MASS INCARCERATION** *are historically linked.*

Contents

8 **From the President**

10 **Foreword**
by Andrea Armstrong

14 Introduction
The Captive State of Louisiana

16 Chapter One
Colonial Foundations

24 Chapter Two
American Transformations

38 Chapter Three
The Convict Lease and Angola

50 Chapter Four
A Blueprint for Mass Incarceration

70 Chapter Five
Breaking Points

92 Epilogue
Reflection and Action

98 **Bibliography**

102 **Acknowledgments**

From the President

THE EXHIBITION *Captive State: Louisiana and the Making of Mass Incarceration* has been revelatory in many ways. During its run at the Historic New Orleans Collection from July 2024 to February 2025, *Captive State* drew national media coverage, a major gift that enabled the production of this very book, and a diverse array of visitors ranging from school groups to entertainers to governmental leaders. The show's ambitious scope and weighty subject matter did not turn people away but rather made our institution an essential stop for thousands of people visiting New Orleans. Popular demand compelled us to extend the show's run beyond its originally scheduled closing date.

But the work of telling this complex story couldn't stop when *Captive State* was deinstalled—and it won't, thanks to the generosity of the Spark Justice Fund at Borealis Philanthropy. After visiting the exhibition, their team, led by Sade Dumas, recognized the value not just in preserving the message of the exhibition but making it available to advocates who would benefit from having its content published as a permanent resource. We are grateful for their support, which underscores a core tenet of HNOC's institutional vision: to invite everyone on our quest to build an equitable and enlightened future.

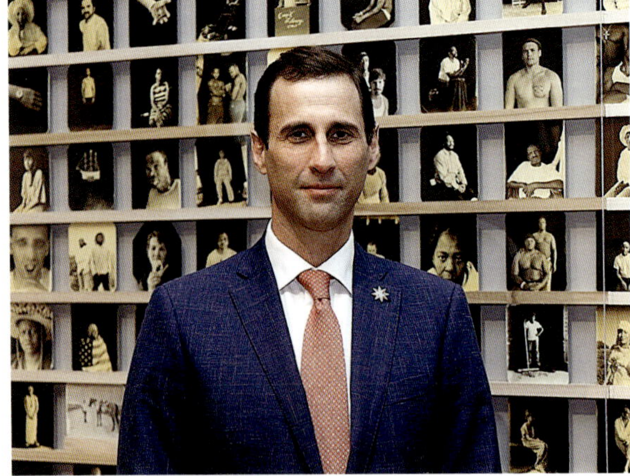

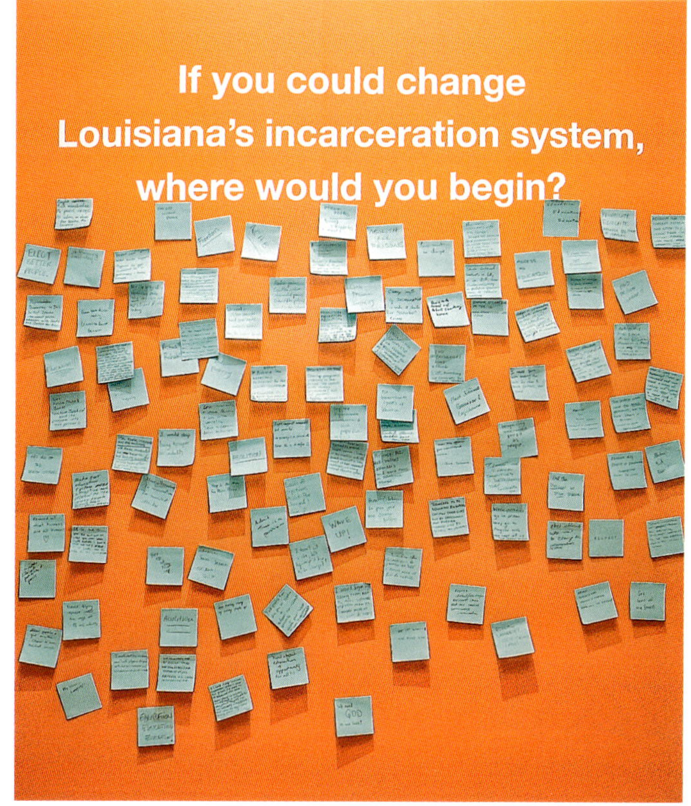

We do mean everyone. During its time at our museum, *Captive State* welcomed in formerly incarcerated people, victim advocates, and law enforcement officials such as Orleans Parish District Attorney Jason Williams and Orleans Parish Sheriff Susan Hutson. We hosted large groups of high school students and teachers, criminal justice reformers, and nonprofit leaders. We even had visits from the likes of singer-songwriter John Legend and Sister Helen Prejean, longtime activist against the death penalty. This wide-ranging audience was in part a product of our intentional efforts to establish meaningful relationships with community partners who could help spread the word about *Captive State*. These partners included an advisory board of six people with a range of experiences with the criminal legal system. They helped our staff shape the content of the exhibition and then performed essential outreach through their own networks. In turn, *Captive State* has drawn attention to the crucial work these people and organizations do themselves.

Their work and the work of *Captive State* continues. Our state remains a global leader in incarceration rates, which disproportionately impact Black Louisianians. *Captive State* charts this phenomenon back to the colonial founding of Louisiana. Though this long history impacts our present circumstances, it does not mean our future has to look the same. Indeed, it should not. We hope that this book serves as a lasting resource.

—DANIEL HAMMER,
HNOC PRESIDENT AND CEO

Captive State concluded in a reflection gallery where visitors could leave their comments on how they would change Louisiana's incarceration system. Photograph by Tere Kirkland, HNOC.

Foreword
Andrea Armstrong

WE HOLD OURSELVES CAPTIVE from greatness through our obsession with incarceration. We cripple ourselves—shortchanging our own potential—by refusing to recognize the humanity of people behind bars. *Captive State: Louisiana and the Making of Mass Incarceration* makes these costs visible, defying conventional accounts that ignore the lived experiences of incarcerated people.

Captive State, through its objective and documentary approach, is the first *full* historical accounting of incarceration in Louisiana. Louisiana has led the nation in incarceration rates *and* murder rates since 1989. If incarceration actually made us safer, we would be the safest state in the United States. Instead, we have spent billions of dollars for the false promise of safety while Louisiana is often last in the nation in every measure of community well-being, including health, education, and economy. This book connects the racist origins of our carceral institutions and practices to our modern-day jails and prisons within the context of what we've sacrificed and lost along the way.

The breadth and depth of *Captive State* is staggering. The exhibition traced over 300 years of Louisiana history, documenting the government's role in operationalizing both chattel slavery and incarceration. Jails and prisons, originally built to hold, discipline, and exploit enslaved and free people, were expanded post–Civil War. Incarceration became the state's preferred tool to legally "establish the supremacy of the white race," as announced at the 1898 constitutional convention. The state legislature created a series of laws that substituted incarceration for enslavement and enhanced the cruel dangers of forced labor that continue today. Private interests continued to profit as the new laws ensured a steady stream of newly freed Black labor.

Captive State is not merely history. Rather, it is evidence of how the past shapes and reverberates within the present. Black Louisianians are still disproportionately incarcerated within dangerous conditions. There is a torturous continuity in descriptions of Louisiana jail and prison conditions. In

INCARCERATION RATES

*Louisiana Compared to Major Countries**

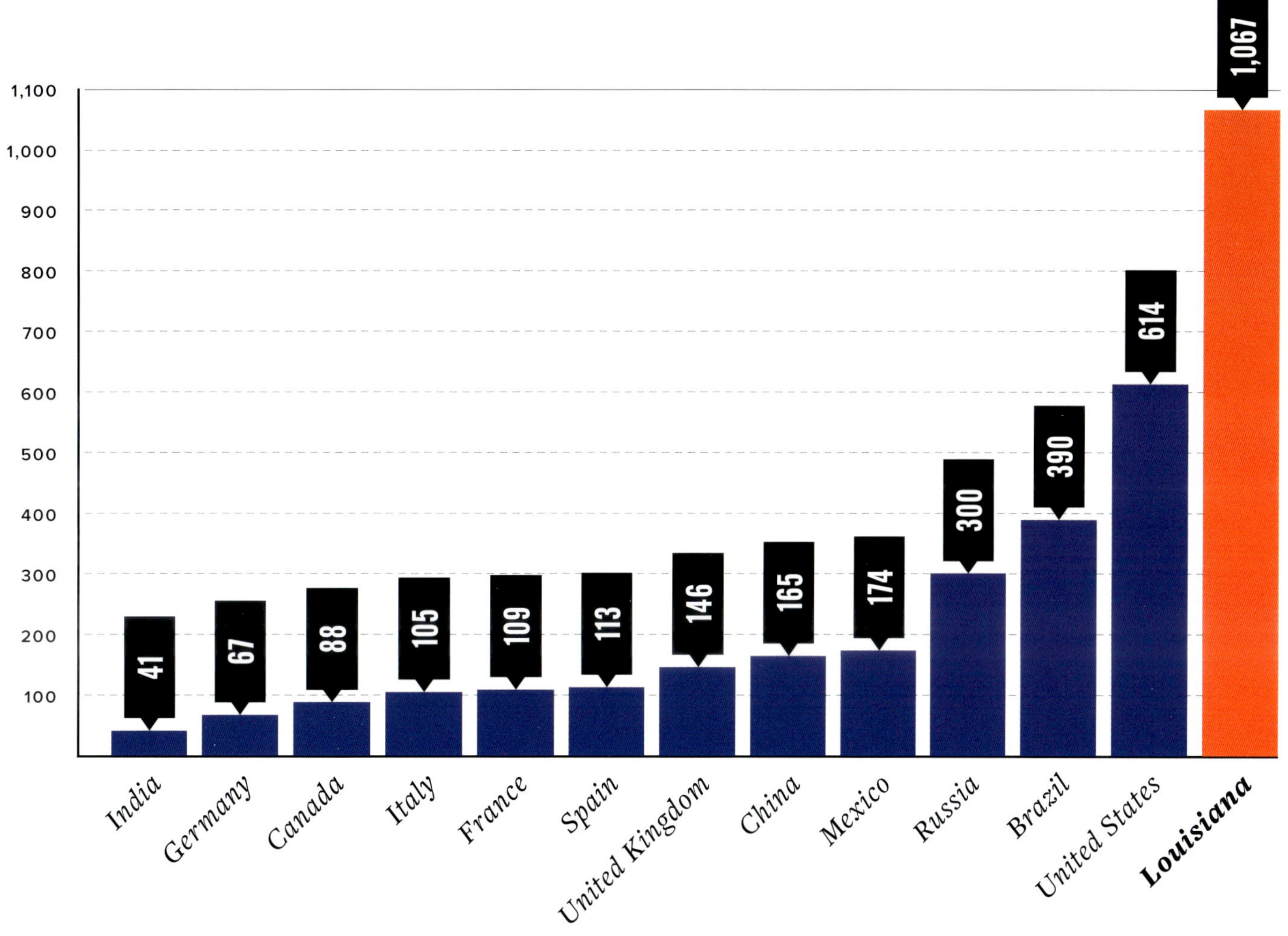

1812, they were described as "wretched"; in 1841 they were "hell"; they were a "shock [to] the conscience" in 1975 and "critically unsafe" in 2018. At the same time, these spaces were expanded and relocated to the margins of our cities and state, hidden from public view, along with the people within them. The exhibition also makes clear the debt that we owe to people incarcerated in the past; their exploitation laid the foundation for today's core infrastructure, including our levees, railroads, and canals. Today, incarcerated people are still forced to work in unsafe conditions for pennies on the dollar, both inside and outside of prisons.

Including the experiences of incarcerated people—both past and present—is a critical element of *Captive State*. History often consists solely of

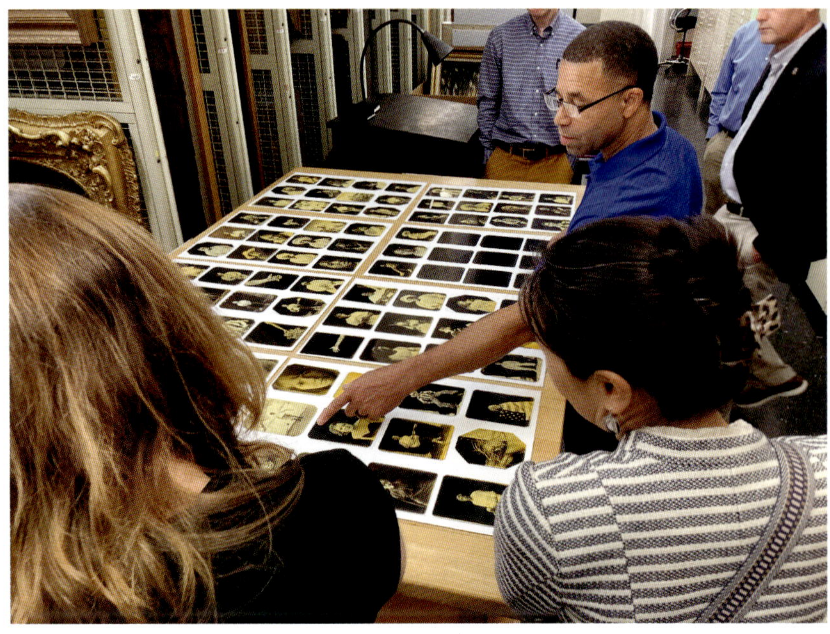

Advisory board member Anthony Hingle Jr. identifies people he knew from Angola while reviewing images featured in *Captive State* with HNOC staff. Photograph by Dave Walker.

records and tales of the powerful, an incomplete and usually self-aggrandizing narrative. Through *Captive State*'s robust documentation, our history of incarceration now includes the extreme costs we impose on our own people and communities. We are confronted with the barbarism of sentencing Peggy in 1820 to drag a thirteen-and-a-half-pound iron ball by her ankle for three years. We read the payment receipts from the jail to enslavers Eliza Farrell and Vincent Roblain in the 1840s for the labor of Rose and Charles on the city chain gang. We witness the scarred heels of men incarcerated at the Louisiana State Penitentiary who, in 1951, slashed their own Achilles tendons with razors to protest brutal working and living conditions at the prison commonly known as Angola. We see Cayne Miceli's purse, which included her asthma medicine, next to a restraint bed similar to the one that she was strapped to in the New Orleans jail when she died in 2009, unable to breathe.

But incarcerated people are not just objects or receptacles for society's hidden punishments. In *Captive State*, they are also a reason for hope. Through their experiences we see the incredible persistence of the human spirit within routinely extreme spaces: the deep kindness, photographed by Lori Waselchuk, etched into the worn faces of Angola's hospice program, which was started by and for incarcerated men; the imagination and creativity of intricately sewn quilts by Gary Tyler, Steven Garner, and other incarcerated men, chronicling redemption and renewal; and the dignity of chefs, mothers, cowboys, fathers, artists, and builders unveiled by Deborah Luster, who took individual photo portraits of hundreds of people in prison from 1998 to 2002. *Captive State* reminds us that currently and formerly incarcerated people led successful efforts to restore dignity and rights to people behind bars, including the right to vote for people on parole and probation and the end of convictions by nonunanimous juries, a racist practice codified in the 1898 Louisiana Constitution.

Neither the harms nor the hope are visible from the outside. Throughout the country, prisons and jails are closed institutions, shielded from public accountability. Jails and prisons rely on this secrecy to enhance their authority and maintain the status quo. To truly grapple with incarceration requires witnessing it firsthand. Over six years, the curators immersed themselves in incarceration history and practices to create an exhibition that serves as a permanent window into these hidden experiences.

In 2019, the *Captive State* curators joined my Loyola law students in a visit to the troubled Jefferson Parish jail. During that visit, they witnessed symptoms of a broken system: overcrowding bodies within tiny walled-off spaces, constant murmurs and shouts from people in physical and mental anguish, and the oppressive anxiety felt by the incarcerated and staff alike. And instead of running away from the complex reality of jails and prisons, curators Eric Seiferth, Kevin T. Harrell, and Katherine Jolliff Dunn dug deeper, visiting the New Orleans jail, the Louisiana State Penitentiary (Angola), and the Louisiana Correctional Institute for Women, as well as documenting the closure of the House of Detention in New Orleans. That dedicated curiosity and openness to learning is what makes *Captive State* so powerful. It is also why the Historic New Orleans Collection (HNOC) team built an incredible advisory board of experts to guide the development of the exhibit.

The *Captive State* advisory board included expertise from Louisiana's two largest organizations led by the formerly incarcerated, Anthony Hingle Jr. from Voice of the Experienced (VOTE) and Montrell Carmouche from Operation Restoration; John Bardes, a historian specializing in slavery, Reconstruction, and early incarceration in Louisiana; Katie Hunter-Lowrey, an organizer and survivor of violence; Jee Park, the executive director of the Innocence Project New Orleans and attorney challenging wrongful convictions and excessive punishment; and myself as an expert on incarceration and the law.

Our advisory board was not simply a token effort, but meaningfully contributed to and refined the hard work of HNOC staff. From 2022 to 2024, during quarterly and then monthly meetings, we helped the curators understand the significance of certain items, like uniforms and restraint cuffs. We helped them engage with these materials respectfully, talking through ways to uplift and visualize the humanity of people incarcerated in our prisons and jails across the state, while also accurately depicting the extreme cruelty within those spaces. The title of the exhibit, suggested by Anthony Hingle Jr., followed hours of debate and discussion. As members of the advisory board, we didn't always agree with one another . . . but we did always challenge each other and HNOC staff to think more deeply about our understanding of incarceration.

And ultimately, this is what the *Captive State* advisory board wants every person who engages with this exhibit—whether in person or within this book—to do. To confront the reality of what is done in our name and to chart a new path forward that reflects our shared humanity. We can choose to do better for ourselves, our communities, and our future. I hope this book reminds us of why we should.

ANDREA ARMSTRONG *is the Dr. Norman C. Francis Distinguished Professor of Law at Loyola University New Orleans College of Law, where she teaches constitutional and criminal law. She is a leading national expert on prison and jail conditions, a 2023 MacArthur Fellow, and an advisory board member for* **Captive State**.

* Widra, *States of Incarceration*. The Louisiana and US rates include people incarcerated in state prisons, local jails, juvenile facilities, Indian Country jails, civil commitment centers, state psychiatric hospitals, federal jurisdictions, Immigration and Customs Enforcement detention centers, and military prisons.

Introduction

THE CAPTIVE STATE OF LOUISIANA

SINCE THE FOUNDING of Louisiana and New Orleans by French colonists, people in power have held others captive as a means of punishment, control, and exploitation. Black Louisianians in particular have been subjugated and forced to labor against their will through chattel slavery and systems of incarceration for more than three hundred years. In the colonial era (1682–1803), the government created systems of enslavement and social caste based on race through legislation, policing, imprisonment, and physical violence. These systems matured after Louisiana was acquired by the United States, and during the first half of the nineteenth century New Orleans became the primary hub of the domestic slave trade.

The United States Congress abolished most forms of slavery when it passed the Thirteenth Amendment to the Constitution in 1865, but it created an exception for the enslavement of people convicted of a crime. This allowed Louisiana to continue a practice begun in 1844 of leasing incarcerated individuals to private citizens and entities for labor on plantations and public infrastructure projects. This practice continued until the turn of the twentieth century and was known as convict leasing. Many incarcerated people were forced to work at a place known as Angola, a property that included several plantations previously owned by one of the largest slave traders in the country. In 1901, the state purchased most of these plantations for the purpose of turning Angola into the permanent home of the Louisiana State Penitentiary. To this day, incarcerated people are forced to labor at Angola for little or no pay in the same fields once worked by enslaved people.

Near the end of the nineteenth century the state ushered in the era of Jim Crow segregation by passing several laws that rendered Black people second-class citizens. One such law that allowed for nonunanimous jury convictions did this work on two levels: it diminished the voices of potential Black jurors, and made it easier to send more Black people to prison. This remained on the books for more than a hundred years and, combined with the "tough-on-crime" policies of more recent decades, caused Louisiana's incarcerated population to explode. Tougher sentencing has led to more people serving life without parole—meaning more people are aging and dying behind bars. And though incarceration rates locally and nationally have begun to decline in recent years, the degree of change is uneven from state to state, and the US remains a global leader in incarceration. Louisiana, for its part, still incarcerates its people at a higher rate than any other state, even as its violent crime rates are in decline. Louisiana's notoriety in this regard is not an accident, but rather a consequence of decisions made by people in power here throughout its history.

Recent years have seen some signs of progress. In 2018, Louisiana voters finally struck down the longstanding nonunanimous jury law. A number of organizations have been formed to advocate for change, fight unjust laws and convictions, and aid people impacted by incarceration. Still, a system cultivated for more than three hundred years does not transform overnight. Moreover, the state remains invested in perpetuating it. In 2025, Louisiana will commit more than a billion dollars to its vast carceral apparatus.

As the human and financial costs continue to mount, Louisiana itself is held captive by this history. This book details how it got to this point, chronicling a three-century arc from its founding as a French colony to the present day.

—ERIC SEIFERTH
AND NICK WELDON

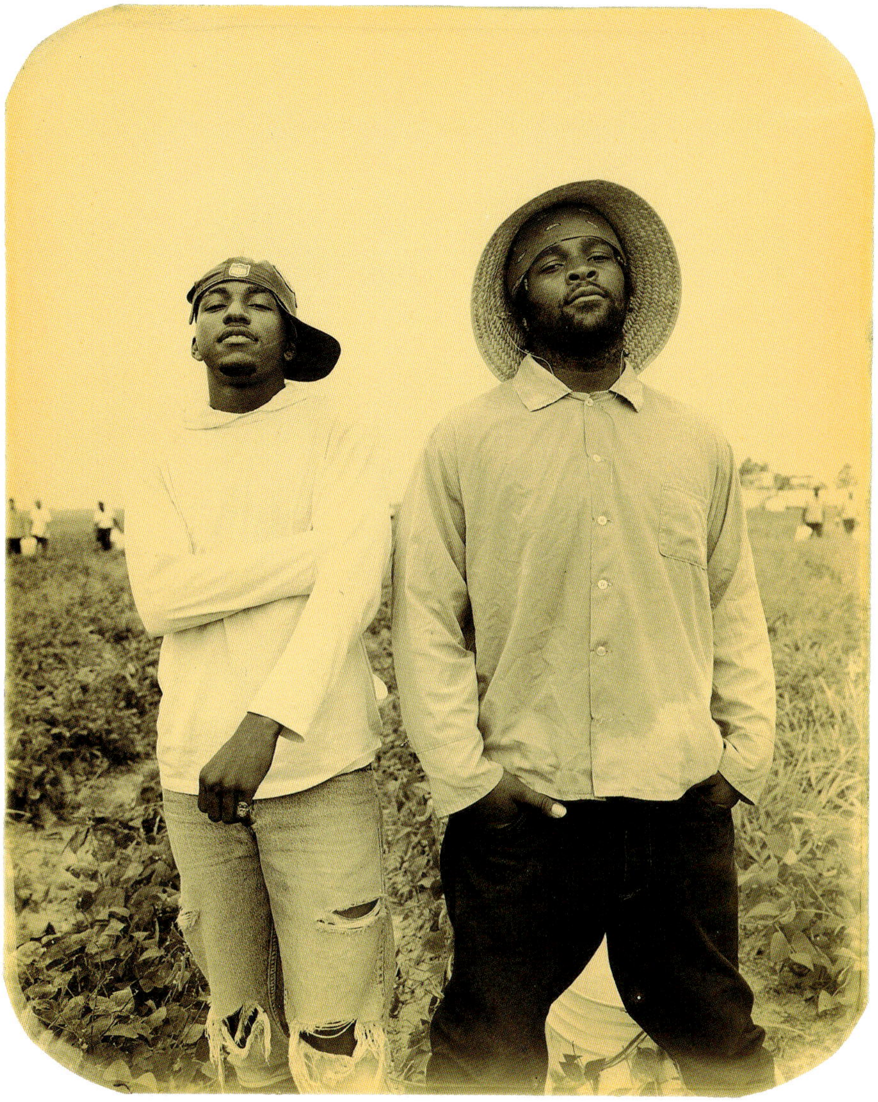

Field Line Workers from ***One Big Self: Prisoners of Louisiana***; 1999; silver emulsion on aluminum; by Deborah Luster; *HNOC, acquisition made possible by the Laussat Society, 2023.0146.1.102*

Chapter One

COLONIAL FOUNDATIONS

"The light is taken from me forever."

—AN OBSERVER OF LOUISIANA'S PRISON CONDITIONS IN 1803[1]

THE SEEDS of the modern criminal legal system were sown during the French and Spanish administrations of the Louisiana colony (1682–1803).

European colonizers instituted a racialized legal system in Louisiana that created a slave society based on white supremacy. Laws, policing, and punishment differed for white residents and those of color, whether free or enslaved, with the most severe outcomes reserved for enslaved men and women. Authorities designed executions to maximize suffering and carried them out in the Place d'Armes, the public plaza now known as Jackson Square.

Throughout this era, officials compelled incarcerated people to perform many jobs that were essential to the development of the colony. French authorities used convict labor to clear cane-

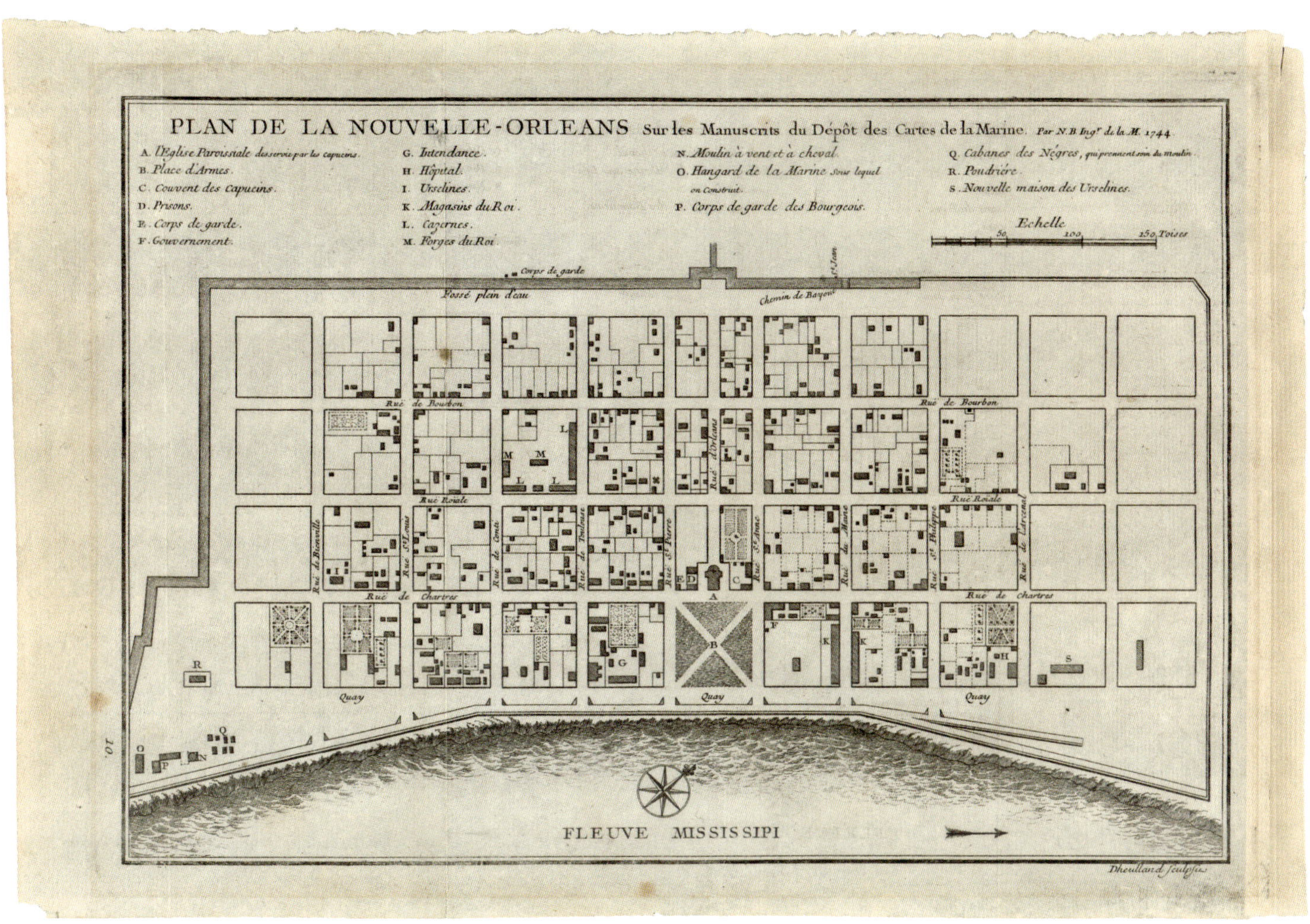

brake on the site that became New Orleans. In the last decades of the eighteenth century, Spanish authorities coerced incarcerated people, many of them also enslaved, into building and maintaining the infrastructure of New Orleans. They regularly performed this labor in public view, from the streets of the French Quarter to the levees surrounding the city.

During these same years, authorities also increased efforts to police enslaved and free people of color. Under French and Spanish rule in Louisiana, Black people in particular lived under close scrutiny and could get swept into a brutal cycle of punishment and exploitation for the slightest indiscretions, as detailed in the following pages.

Plan de la Nouvelle-Orleans; 1744; by Jacques Nicolas Bellin, cartographer; Guillame Dheulland, engraver; *HNOC, gift of Patrick Henley, 2011.0377*

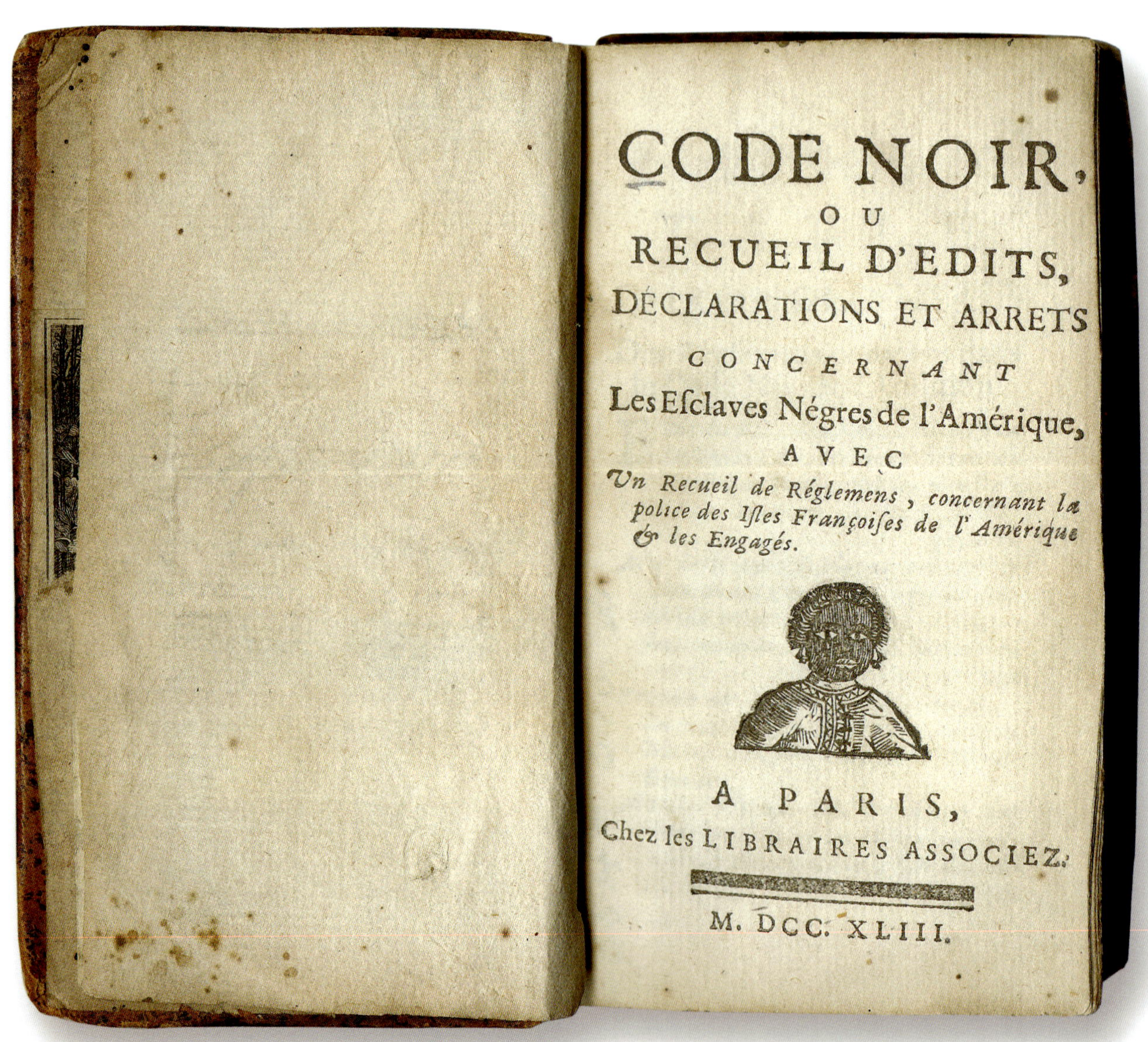
CODE NOIR,
OU
RECUEIL D'EDITS,
DÉCLARATIONS ET ARRETS
CONCERNANT
Les Esclaves Négres de l'Amérique,
AVEC
Un Recueil de Réglemens, concernant la police des Isles Françoises de l'Amérique & les Engagés.

A PARIS,
Chez les LIBRAIRES ASSOCIEZ.

M. DCC. XLIII.

Code noir; Paris: Libraires associez, 1743; *HNOC, 80-654-RL*

THE CODE NOIR

FRENCH COLONIAL LOUISIANA was founded with a set of laws known as Le code noir de la Louisiane (the Black code of Louisiana). First issued by the French Crown in 1724, the code consisted of fifty-five articles restricting the lives of enslaved and free people of African descent as well as religious minorities.

These laws created and maintained a racially segregated society based on white supremacy that utilized highly visible physical violence as a principal form of punishment. The following excerpts from the code typify its standards for crime and punishment:

> *We forbid slaves belonging to different masters to gather in crowds. . . . We command all our subjects to seize such offenders, and to arrest and conduct them to prison.*
>
> —CODE NOIR, ARTICLE 13

> *The slave who has struck his master, his mistress, the husband of his mistress, or their children . . . shall be put to death.*
>
> —CODE NOIR, ARTICLE 27

> *The runaway slave who has remained at large for one month . . . shall have his ears cut off, and shall be branded with the fleur-de-lis on one shoulder.*
>
> —CODE NOIR, ARTICLE 32

The Superior Council, the French colony's main governing body, oversaw all aspects of the criminal legal system, with the Code noir guiding its rulings. Punishment in colonial Louisiana was often violent, and executions were frequently carried out in public. Colonial authorities also made use of physical torture during interrogation and as penalty for a wide range of offenses, including escaping enslavement. The stories of Cezar and Jeannette in this chapter are representative of many cases in the Superior Council records.

In 1751 the Superior Council issued a series of thirty-one *réglements* (regulations) that tightened control over enslaved people's movements and empowered white citizens to help police the enslaved population. Examples of these laws include:

> ARTICLE 19 *We cannot too strongly recommend that all citizens be less lenient toward them [the enslaved], and punish them accordingly on every occasion.*

> ARTICLE 23 *Any negro who shall be found in the public streets and roads, carrying . . . a cane, whip, or baton, shall be struck by the first white [man] who finds him.*

> ARTICLE 27 *Any negro or other slave who shall be stopped in the streets or roads at night without a note from his master shall be on the spot taken to prison.*

To aid in the enforcement of colonial laws, New Orleans opened its first jail in 1730, adjacent to the Place d'Armes, where most punishments took place. French scientist, architect, and engineer Pierre Baron is credited with designing the building. The jail was the first brick structure of which there is record in the city. The watercolor on the next page includes elevations of the front and rear facades of the building, as well as floor plans indicating the locations of the *cour* (jail yard), *chambre criminel* (criminal courtroom), *chambre du consierge* (jailer's quarters), *cachot* (dungeon), and *chambres* (cells).[2]

THE SPANISH ERA

SPAIN TOOK CONTROL of Louisiana in 1768 and soon replaced the Code noir with its own edicts governing the lives

PROFILES

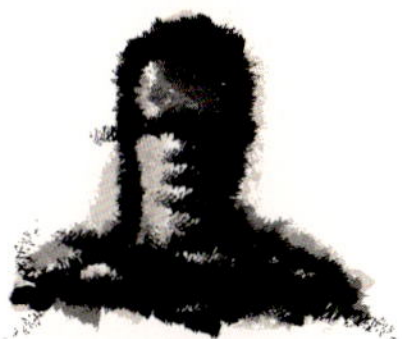

CEZAR

An enslaved man named Cezar confessed to multiple crimes following an interrogation that involved torture. He was found guilty of theft and wounding a white citizen with a gun, in violation of Code noir laws against theft (Article 29), carrying weapons (Article 12), and assaults against free persons (Article 28). A judge imposed a sentence that included doing penance at the church, having his right hand cut off with an axe, and having his limbs broken with a mallet while on a "breaking wheel" in the public square. Cezar's broken body was raised on a pole overlooking Bayou Road and allowed to be "finished off" by the sun, flies, and birds.

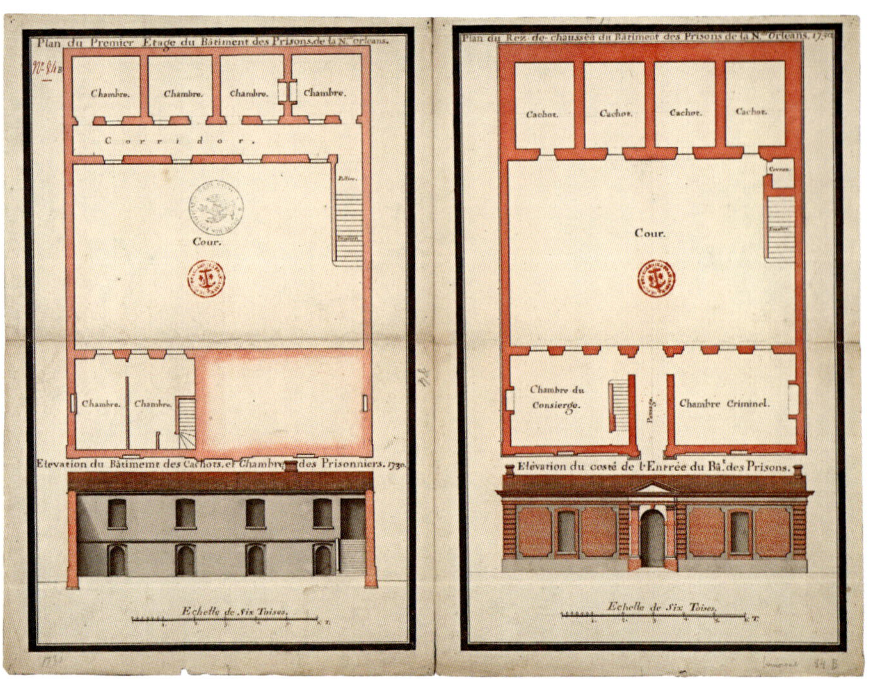

of people of color in the colony. The Spanish, under the leadership of Governor Alejandro O'Reilly, demolished the old French prison in 1769 and in its place constructed a new municipal government building, now called the Cabildo. Located next to St. Louis Cathedral and originally called the Casa Capitular, the Cabildo housed administrative and judicial meeting rooms, jailer's quarters, and the civil and military prisons for the colony.

Front and rear elevations and floorplan for the New Orleans prison; January 14, 1730; watercolor on paper; *courtesy of Archives Nationales d'Outre-Mer*

The Cabildo jail was unsanitary, damp, crowded, and crawling with vermin. "Under the Spanish government [the jail] was a wretched receptacle of vice and misery," wrote Major Amos Stoddard in an 1812 history of that era. "Like the grave it received many tenants, who were soon forgotten by the world."[3] It was renovated during the last years of Spanish rule in Louisiana. These investments in expanding and improving the facility were made following devastating fires in 1788 and 1794 that ravaged large sections of the city, including the jail complex. Work was completed in 1801.

During the era of Spanish rule in New Orleans, colonial authorities continued to have incarcerated and enslaved people perform municipal

PROFILES

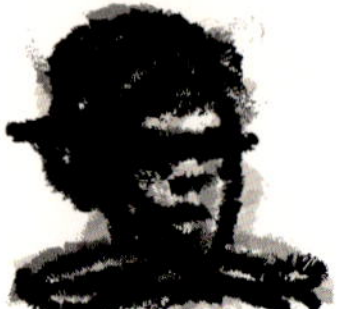

JEANNETTE

In September 1746, the Superior Council called Jeannette, a free woman of color, to answer for the crime of hosting supper parties at her home in New Orleans for groups of enslaved people. The Superior Council cited Article 13 from the Code noir, which forbade the gathering of enslaved people, and warned her to discontinue the gatherings or face punishment. A few months later, Jeannette appears in court records again on charges of theft and unpaid debts. The Superior Council condemned her to enslavement, likely because the council believed she was helping enslaved people to escape.

labor. From the streets of the French Quarter to the levees surrounding the city, incarcerated and enslaved people built and maintained the growing city. These people were forced to carry out numerous responsibilities, including constructing and maintaining sewers, levees, and streets. They built the Carondelet Canal, the largest infrastructure project undertaken by the Spanish in New Orleans.[4]

On June 1, 1795, Spanish governor Luis Héctor, barón de Carondelet issued a decree in response to a revolution led by enslaved people in Saint Domingue and two attempted uprisings of enslaved people in Pointe Coupee, Louisiana. The decree included a series of ordinances that increased policing of both the system of slavery and those enslaved. The laws expanded the policing powers of citizen patrols in newly created districts, each under the control of an appointed official with a vested interest in surveilling and limiting the mobility and activities of enslaved people. Meanwhile, jailers and police worked hand in hand with enslavers to capture enslaved people who had escaped and to incarcerate and punish them, with enslavers reimbursing the government for the costs of incarceration. This cycle of surveillance, punishment, and exploitation would continue into the early American era.

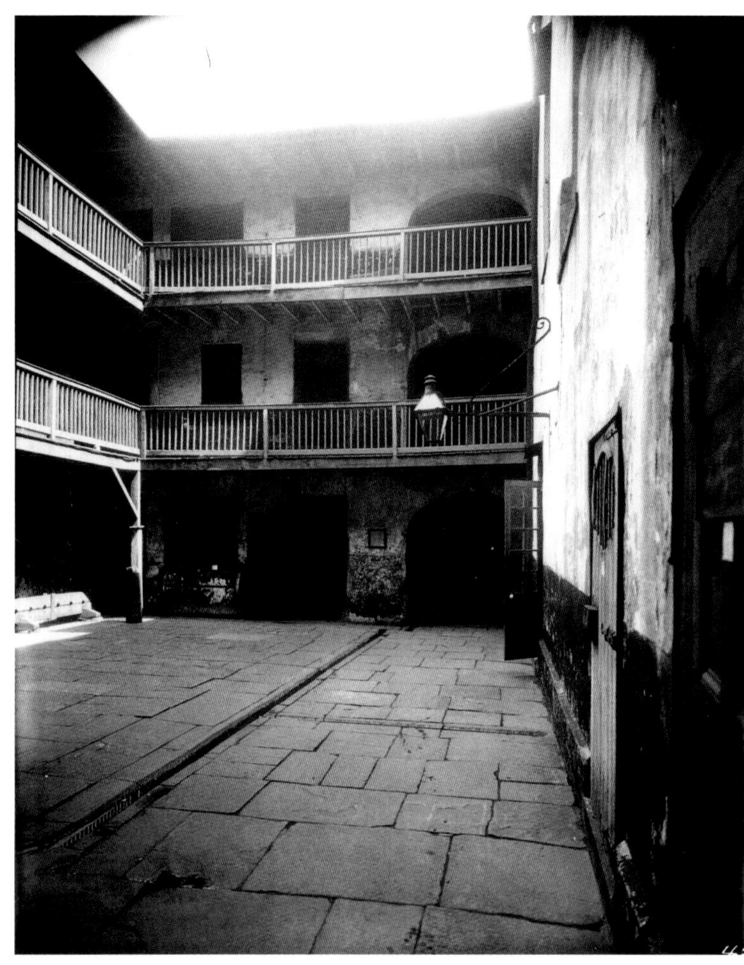

Cabildo jail courtyard; between 1930 and 1939; photograph by Charles L. Franck Photographers; *Charles L. Franck Studio Collection at HNOC, 1979.325.3462*

1 Roberts, "Edward Livingston," 1040. The quotation has been translated and originates from an 1804 manuscript by a French visitor to New Orleans named Paul Alliot, who wrote: "If the most peaceful inhabitant, who offends a magistrate or a rich man, does not flee promptly, he is cast for life into a dungeon without being enabled to learn the reasons for it. He can be assured that there exists no guaranty for him. He can not even procure defense. All communication is forbidden him. He can say as he enters the prison, 'The light is taken from me forever.'"

2 Wilson, *Architecture of Colonial Louisiana*, 16.

3 Stoddard, *Sketches*, 154.

4 Din and Harkins, *New Orleans Cabildo*, 247–57; Acts and Deliberations of the Cabildo, 1769–1803. Cabildo entries of note: December 9, 1769; March 16, 1770; April 29, 1785; March 9, 1792; and July 15 and November 3, 1796.

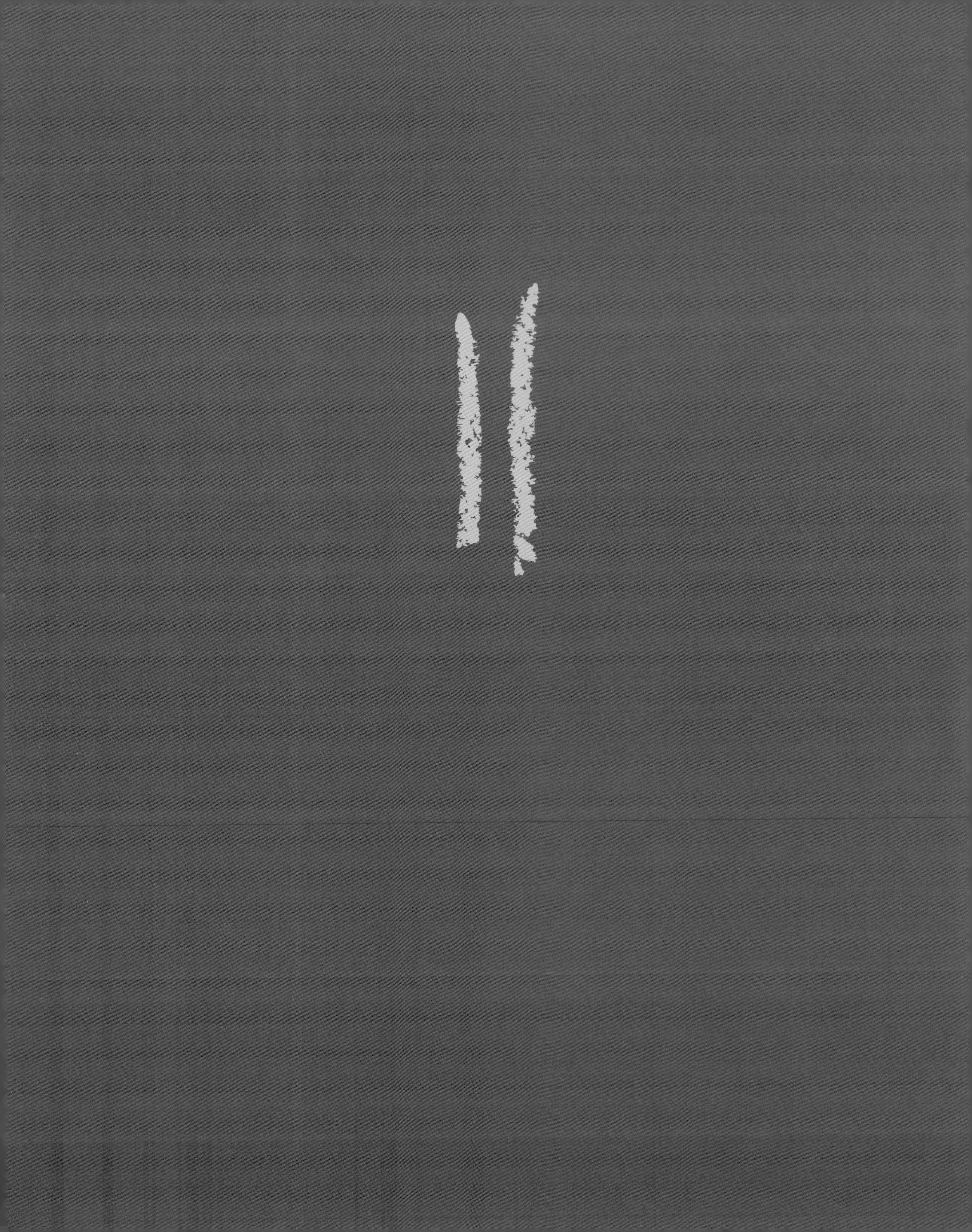

Chapter Two

AMERICAN TRANSFORMATIONS

"We are in a country of slaves."

—NEW ORLEANS MAYOR JOHN WATKINS DESCRIBING THE NEED FOR A POLICE FORCE, 1805[1]

UNDER AMERICAN CONTROL, the systems of slavery and incarceration continued to be mutually reinforcing in New Orleans.

In the decades that followed the Louisiana Purchase of 1803, New Orleans became the principal site of the country's domestic slave trade, and the number of enslaved people in the city reached unprecedented levels. During this time, the city used incarceration to help control enslaved Black people and maintain white supremacy.

This transition to American governance coincided with the end of the Haitian Revolution, a successful rebellion by the enslaved population in the French colony of Saint Domingue, which eventually sent some 10,000 émigrés to Louisiana. Fears of similar uprisings led to the creation of a municipal police force in New Orleans. Formed in 1805, the force was primarily focused on controlling the city's large population of enslaved people. Dressed in blue, officers carried weapons and patrolled the streets. White and free Black refugees from Saint Domingue who had made their way to New Orleans were among the city's first policemen. In a new country and with limited employment opportunities, members of this community were willing to take the low-paying job that serving on the force offered.

The same year the police force was created, New Orleans began using a system of police jails to house and punish enslaved people. Capturing people escaping enslavement was a core responsibility of the police. A significant number of free people of color misidentified as escapees were also incarcerated in police jails. In 1830—a typical year under this system—one in five Black New Orleanians was sent to the police jail. The ratio was even higher for the enslaved, who were jailed at a rate of one in three.[2]

Runaway Slave—Runaway from the subscriber No 221 Magazine three weeks ago the negro woman slave named SOPHIA, aged 27 years, about 5 ft high, marked with the small pox, crooked feet; big lips, wants some teeth before, was dressed when she started with a blue spotted domestic frock, she is well known in suburb St Mary as a washer by the day, and is supposed to have been harboured in said suburb.

Ten dollars reward will be given for the apprehension and delivery to the subscriber of said slave or for lodging the same in the jail of New Orleans.

m 31-3t P. SHIELD.

FIFTEEN DOLLARS REWARD.

Run away from the subscriber, Esplanade corner of Rampart street, on the 28th inst, the negro girl SARAH, 19 years, 5 fhet 2 inches high, she has a sulky look when spoken to; when she left was dressed in a light purple and spotted calico frock. She has a large scar between her shoulders. The above reward will be paid to whomsoever will will apprehend said slave and lodge her in the parish jail of New Orleans.

mar 31 JAMES FINLAY.

NOTICE—Detained in the jail of the parish of Jefferson, a negro boy who calls himself John, is about 12 years old, and says he belongs to Mr Williams. Also a mullatto boy called, Anfield, 14 years old who says he belongs to Mr Bouligny. The owners are requested to claim them in conformity with the law. J. CHARBONNET,

m 29 Sheriff of the parish of Jefferson.

$10 REWARD.—Ran away from her mistress on Monday morning, the 17th instant, the negro woman SUSAN, about 22 years old, very black, low in stature, but rather stout built, round face, appears to be diffident when spoken to and in speaking exhibits the broken English dialect of the African raised in Charleston, S. C., where the race associate much together, and from whence she was brought but a few months since. The above reward will be paid for her delivery at the Jail of the Second Municipality by application at No. 37 Natchez st.

Feb. 25—6t

$100 REWARD,

Will be paid for the apprehension and delivery of the following described slave in any jail of the state: FREDERICK, *alias* FRED, a griffe, about 30 years old, 5 feet 11 inches high, good looking, has but little beard, and has lost an upper front tooth; is well known in the city, having driven a dray for the last ten years. He ranaway on the evening of the 28th inst. It is supposed that he has taken away with him his wife, a black woman, belonging to Mr. C. Genois. He has likewise taken away a female child of his, about 6 or 7 years old, very smart for her age, and cuppled.

may 31 6td&2tW FRERET BROTHERS.

Notices of people who escaped enslavement (compiled reproductions):

Advertisements for Sophia, Sarah, and John; from the *New Orleans Bee*, April 2, 1836; *HNOC, 1974.25.23.6.3*

Advertisement for Susan; from the *New Orleans Daily Picayune*, February 25, 1845; *courtesy of City Archives and Special Collections, New Orleans Public Library*

Advertisement for Frederick; from the *New Orleans Daily Picayune*, May 31, 1840; *courtesy of City Archives and Special Collections, New Orleans Public Library*

One in five Black New Orleanians was sent to the police jail at some point during the year 1830.

The first police jail was within the Cabildo jail complex. Its conditions were described in Gustave de Beaumont and Alexis de Tocqueville's 1833 book, *On the Penitentiary System in the United States and its Application in France*: "Examining the prison of New Orleans, we found men together with hogs, in the midst of all odors and nuisances. In locking up the criminals, nobody thinks of rendering them better, but only of taming their malice; they are put in chains like ferocious beasts; and instead of being corrected, they are rendered brutal."[3]

Enslaved people who were arrested were held in police jails until an enslaver paid the costs for housing, food, clothing, any medical services rendered, and fees for inflicting punishment. Through police jails, New Orleans in its American era expanded its control over the Black population and developed a model for the rest of the South.

CHAIN GANGS AND FORCED LABOR

NEW ORLEANS RELIED on forced labor from incarcerated and enslaved people with increased regularity. For public infrastructure projects city authorities used chain gangs—groups of enslaved and incarcerated people forced to work while wearing chains. The practice of using chain gangs for public works developed in the Caribbean and was likely introduced to the United States via New Orleans. Chain gangs became integral to building and maintaining the rapidly growing city.

Male chain gangs were used to build and repair roads and sewers, widen the river, fortify levees, dig graves for

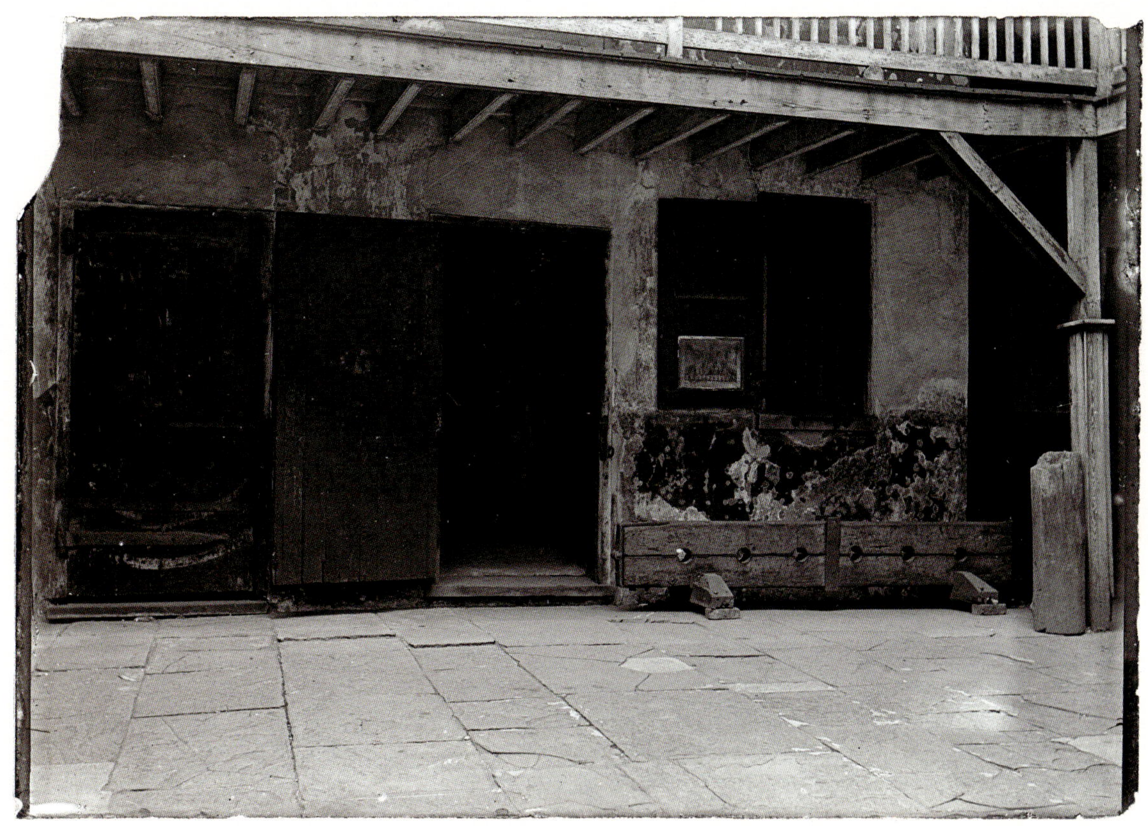

STATE-SANCTIONED TORTURE

Foot stocks (seen at right in the image above) restrained an individual's feet and functioned as a form of corporal punishment and public humiliation. The subject's ankles were set in the holes, then the extremely heavy hinged wooden boards were closed and secured, preventing escape. The restrained individual was subject to all manner of public torment from passersby, including verbal insults, kicking, punching, whipping, and the dumping of refuse. Using foot stocks as a form of public punishment on incarcerated white people was abolished by the Louisiana legislature in 1827, but enslaved individuals continued to be subjected to this torture until sometime in the 1840s. Many of the city's jails used foot stocks within their interior courtyards as punishment throughout the nineteenth century.[4]

Cabildo courtyard; between 1928 and 1940; glass plate negative by Dan Leyrer; *HNOC, gift of Allan Phillip Jaffe, 1981.324.1.40*

"The shame and the humiliation they would experience in . . . these laborious duties would serve as a greater punishment, more keenly felt than even the prison or the lash."

—MAYOR NICHOLAS GIROD TO THE NEW ORLEANS CITY COUNCIL, MAY 8, 1813

cemeteries, and assist in emergency aid. They built the city's first parish prison and were responsible for its daily maintenance. Enslaved and incarcerated women were used to keep streets and gutters clean and clear of debris. By midcentury, chain gangs were widely used, and the details of their work on New Orleans infrastructure projects were recorded daily in city surveyor logbooks.

The relationship between the City of New Orleans and enslavers is also laid bare in receipts and promissory notes, which identified the enslaved person, enslaver, number of days the enslaved person was forced to work, their per-day pay, and the total amount owed or paid to the enslaver. Some examples of these transactions include:

> $1.50 paid to the enslaver Eliza Farrell for eight days of chain-gang labor performed by an enslaved woman named Rose

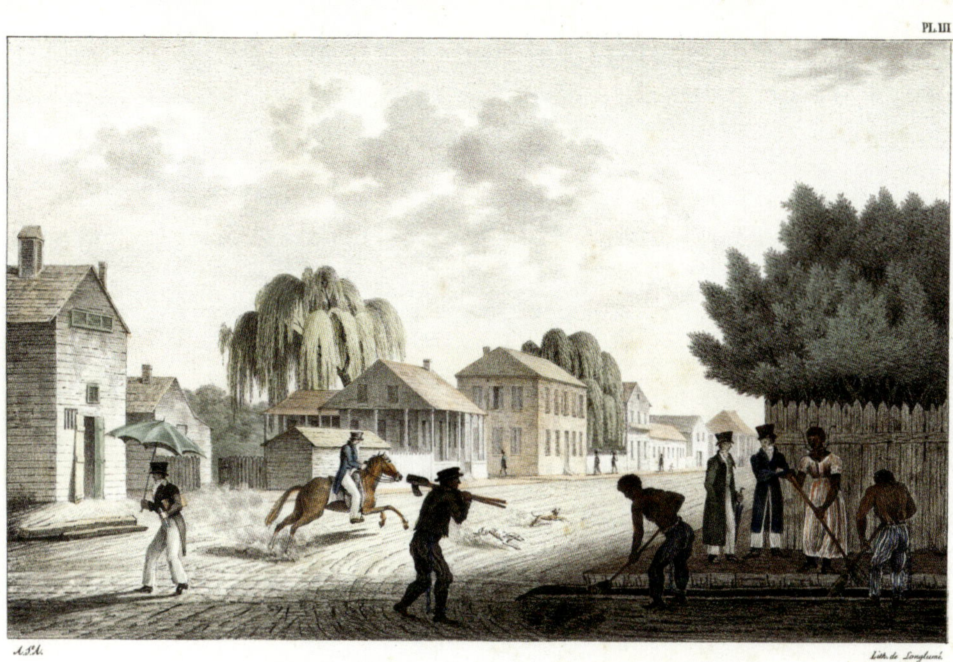

Vue d'une rue du Faubourg Ste Marie. Nelle Orléans.
(Louisiane)

PUBLIC PUNISHMENT

In the darkened foreground of the lithograph above, four enslaved individuals are shown cleaning a gutter in the newly developed Faubourg St. Marie, today's Central Business District. The three men are in chains, and the woman is wearing an iron collar, which was typically used as punishment for an attempted escape. Also of note are the clothes they are wearing. City officials required incarcerated Black workers to wear brightly colored uniforms (reddish pink for women, blue for men) to shame and distinguish them from their white counterparts, who wore civilian dress.

Vue d'une Rue du Faubourg Ste. Marie, Nelle. Orléans. (Louisiane); ca. 1821; lithograph with watercolor by Felix Achille de Beaupoil Saint-Aulaire, artist; P. Langlume, lithographer; *HNOC, L. Kemper and Leila Moore Williams Founders Collection, 1937.2.3*

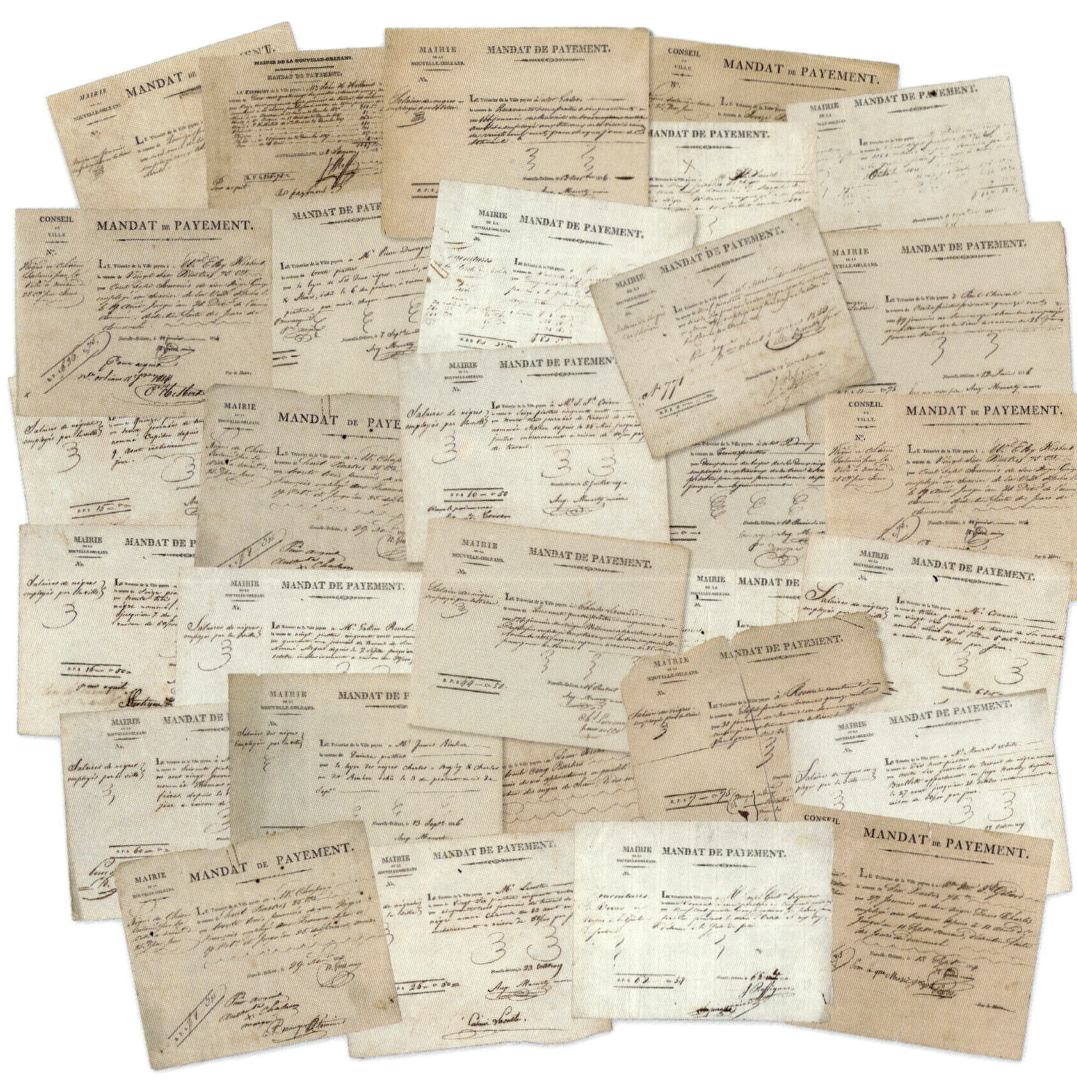

Image compiled from receipts and promissory notes between the City of New Orleans and enslavers; 1813–42; compilation by Cecilia Moscardó; *HNOC, MSS 44.7.1–.17; 70-80-L.11; 76-143-L; 2015.0513.10; 2016.0357; 2016.0408.1–.2*

$2.44 promised to the enslaver Vincent Roblain for thirteen days of chain-gang labor performed by an enslaved man named Charles

$64.75 paid to the enslaver Meilleur for 257 days of chain-gang labor performed by an enslaved man named Thomas

Today, people incarcerated in Louisiana are paid between $0.02 and $1.00 per hour, with the vast majority earning less than $0.20 hourly.[5]

In addition to paying enslavers for the labor of the individuals they enslaved, the city also provided a fixed sum to the jail operator each month to cover the costs associated with feeding and housing them until the enslavers reimbursed the jail for those expenses. Those were not the only reasons an enslaver might request payment from the city. In one case, an enslaver named

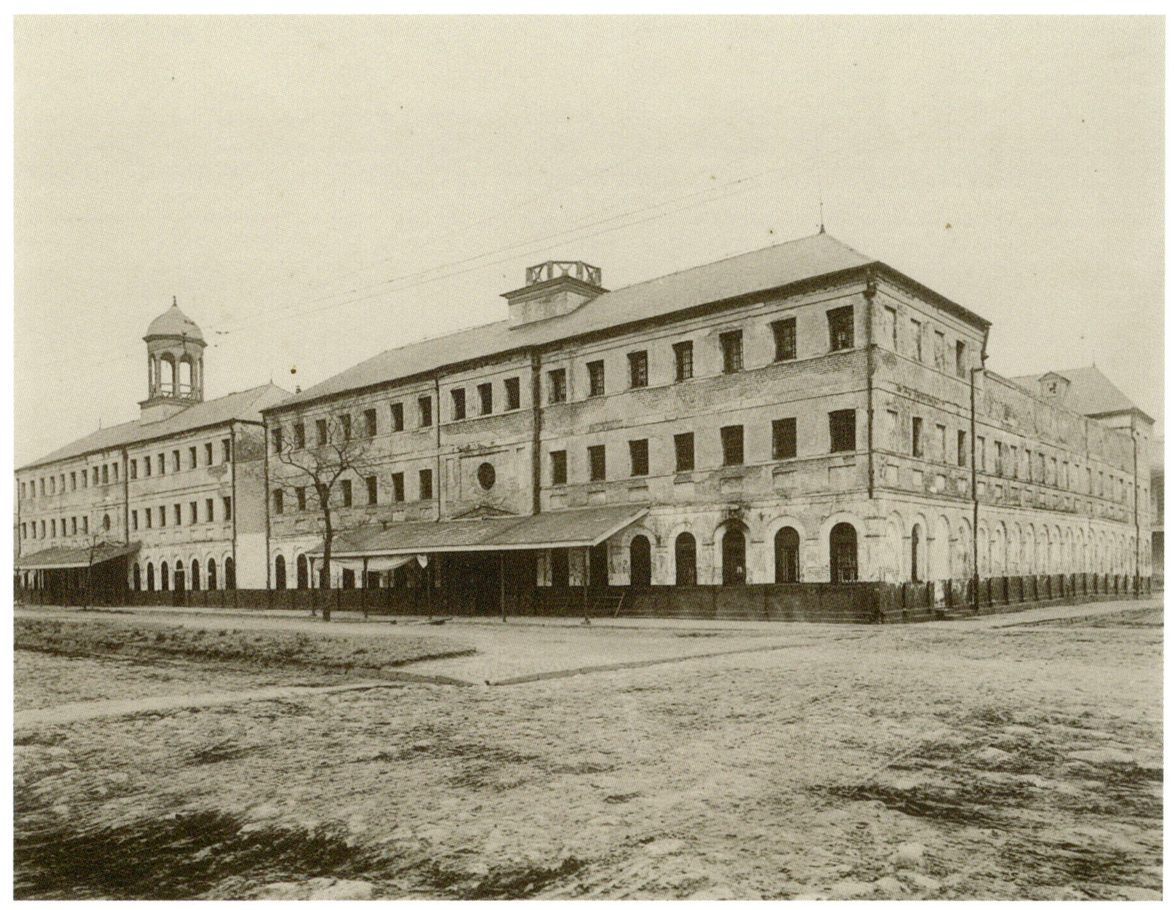

Chardon sent Phibie, a woman he enslaved, to a police jail for punishment. Mayor Nicholas Girod placed her on a chain gang for two years, and, afterward, Chardon demanded restitution from the city for the poor physical condition in which she was returned.

AN EARLY ERA OF MASS INCARCERATION

FROM 1820 TO 1830, the rate of Black New Orleanians being jailed nearly doubled, from around one in ten being incarcerated at some point in 1820 to one in five in 1830. As New Orleans began jailing more of its Black population, officials also dramatically increased the size and number of incarceration facilities across the city.[6]

Most prominent among these was the First Parish Prison, which opened in 1834.[7] The facility was built on Orleans Street in Tremé, one of the oldest African American neighbor-

The Old Parish Prison; from *Art Work of New Orleans* (Chicago: W. H. Parish Publishing Co., 1895); *HNOC, 1974.25.3.246*

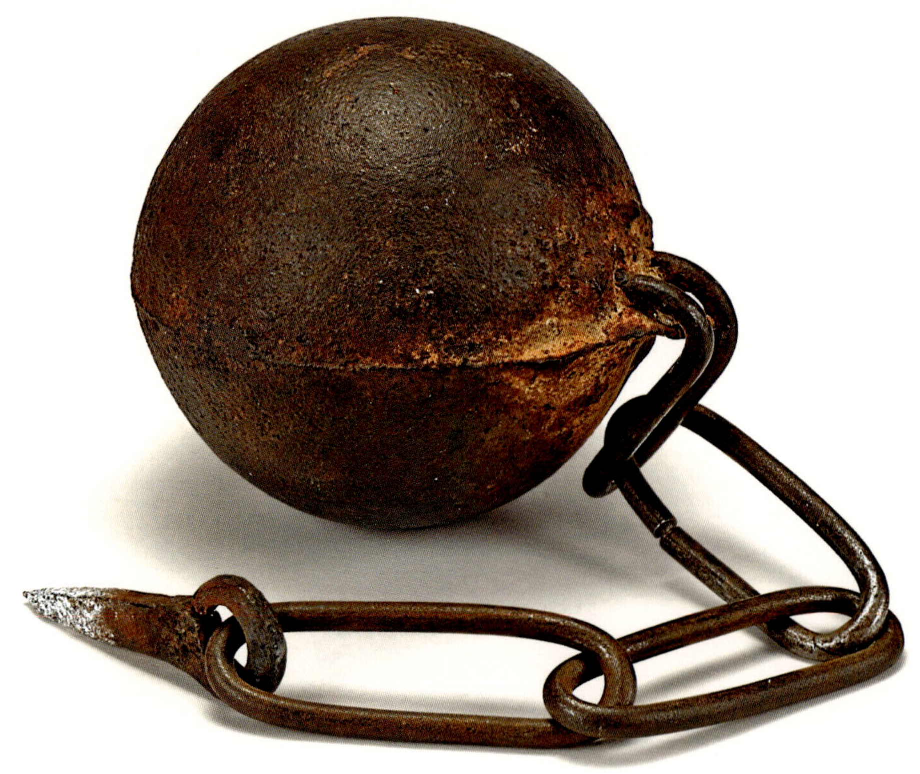

Iron ball and chain worn by Peggy; ca. 1820; *HNOC, 90-58-L.3.1; MSS 44.5.12*

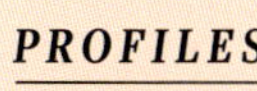

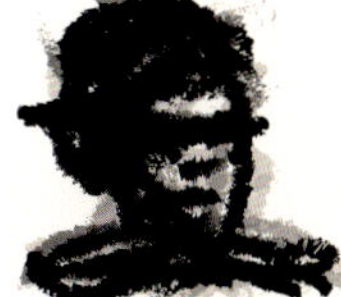

PEGGY

On the night of July 9, 1820, Peggy, an enslaved woman on a plantation in St. John the Baptist Parish, walked to a neighboring plantation and confronted another enslaved woman, Madelaine, about two dresses she had loaned her that had been returned in tatters. The encounter resulted in Peggy fatally stabbing a different enslaved woman in the chest.

The court found Peggy guilty of manslaughter. Her punishment was to receive thirty-nine lashes and to work "at the service of [her] master" for three years with a thirteen-and-a-half-pound iron ball attached to her leg. A shackle or ring, now lost, would have been used to fasten the heavy weight to Peggy's ankle.

hoods in the United States. Moving the jail from the Cabildo to Tremé allowed for a larger complex—one that was further from the city center and less visible.

Like the Cabildo jail it replaced, the parish prison was racially segregated. People incarcerated at the facility routinely endured physical violence administered by the state. Jail officials regularly whipped enslaved people incarcerated here and also carried out executions at the site. According to the *Daily Picayune*, reviewing the history of the building in 1895: "The parish prison was . . . the place where refractory slaves were sent to receive a dose of cat o'nine tails, or to be confined in the dungeons, with stocks on their feet, and in extreme cases the rebellious blacks were kept immured in the dark cells on a diet of bread and water until reduced to the proper degree of submission."[8]

By 1850 roughly a dozen facilities were incarcerating people in New Orleans, not counting the many spaces where enslaved men and women were held captive and punished by individual enslavers and slave traders. Police jails continued to confine enslaved people and free people of color wrongfully identified as enslaved, as well as free Black sailors, whose freedom of movement frightened southern officials as a threat to the system of slavery. Authorities could hold people captive in police jails without judicial procedure, require them to perform manual labor, and subject them to brutally violent punishments. People held in a police jail could only leave if a free person claimed custodianship of them.

New Orleans June the 18 1841

Honrable Jacob Barker

Sir I have Lain in this
Prison 6 mounth, and now am sick and have nothing
to healp my self with and cannot hear or get my
papers from my Native place and as I have been a
waiting to hare from you or see you as you and Mr
Smith took my Name three mounth, ago as a Free man
and informd me that you would see to my case and I have
not heard from you since and had no chance to write you sir
I embrace this time to inform you that I am a stranger
hear and came hear in the Ship Shead of Boston and
was taken on the eve of her sailing for Boston and
had no papers but my Protection the capt being a stran
ger to me and this Place **could do nothing to release me
from Hell** as I may call it I most humbly beg you sir com
see me or send me an answar for we are Stowed away
hear like smugled goods and if sick we may Die for a
frind or healp I belong to Connecticut born in the Tow
of Lisbon County of New London and do not know
hoo to write untill I see you Sir I Pray you in the Name
of God to call and see me soon as you get this and then
I will inform you All

Sir Your Moste Humble Servt

Rufus Kinsman

Rufus Kinsman

Letter from Rufus Kinsman to attorney Jacob Barker (emphasis added); June 18, 1841; blue ink on paper; *courtesy of Rhode Island Historical Society, Rowland G. and Caroline Newbold Hazard Papers*

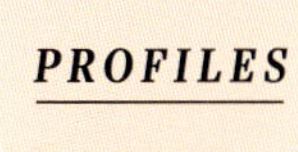

PROFILES

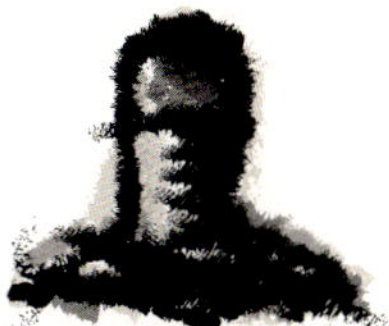

RUFUS KINSMAN

On December 24, 1840, Rufus Kinsman, a free Black sailor on shore leave in New Orleans, was set to return home to Boston when police suddenly arrested him under the charge that he was a fugitive slave. The police ignored Kinsman's identity papers proving his status as a free man and locked him in a police jail. For thirteen months, Kinsman was whipped and forced to labor on a city chain gang.

Kinsman managed to smuggle letters to a lawyer working to help release men like himself mistakenly imprisoned as fugitive slaves. A full seven months after this letter, the police released Kinsman into the custody of a ship captain headed toward Liverpool.[9]

White residents convicted of petty crimes were sent to city workhouses, which like police jails used forced labor, though it was performed within the walls of the workhouse rather than in public view on city streets. Additionally, guardhouses with temporary holding cells, akin to today's police stations, existed across the city.

During the Civil War, the city consolidated its network of police jails and workhouses into a single facility, the City Workhouse, that held incarcerated men and women in spaces segregated by race and gender.

Under American rule, Louisiana officials built upon the methods of control and punishment deployed by their colonial predecessors. This included further differentiating the treatment of incarcerated people on the basis of race. White people were, increasingly, to be "rehabilitated" behind closed doors. Black people in the system were to be "corrected" through physical violence and forced labor still carried out in public view, whether they were housed in city jails or, increasingly after the Civil War, at the state prison upriver.

---

1 Carter, *Territorial Papers*, 503.

2 1830 US Census for New Orleans as published in Wade, *Slavery in the Cities*, 326; daily admittance data from City Police Jail "Daily Reports," as cited in Bardes, "Mass Incarceration," 65–69.

3 De Beaumont and de Tocqueville, *On the Penitentiary System*, 13.

4 Huber and Wilson, *The Cabildo*, 85.

5 Louisiana Department of Public Safety and Corrections, Department Regulation No. AM-C-1, "Offender Incentive Pay and Other Wage Compensation," September 12, 2021.

6 Bardes, "Mass Incarceration," 65–69.

7 Despite its name, the facility was a jail. Typically, jails are designed for short-term detention and prisons are where people convicted of higher-level offenses serve their sentences. New Orleans has traditionally called its primary jail a prison—a practice that continued into the twentieth and twenty-first centuries.

8 "From the Old Parish Prison to the New Jail," *Daily Picayune* (New Orleans), January 18, 1895.

9 Bardes, "Sailing While Black."

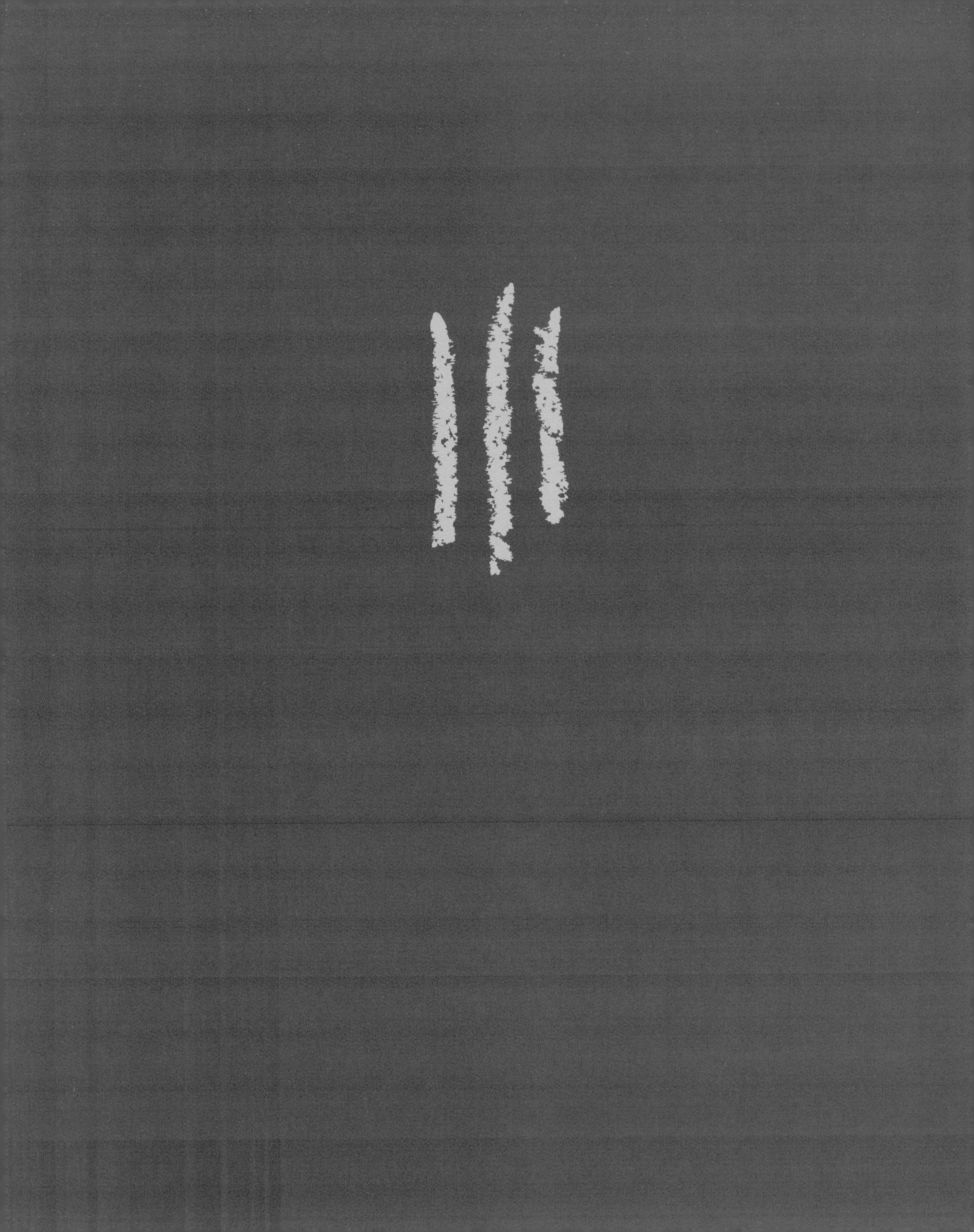

Chapter Three

THE CONVICT LEASE AND ANGOLA

"These convicts, we don't own 'em. One dies, get another."

—UNNAMED LESSEE AT NATIONAL PRISON ASSOCIATION MEETING, 1883[1]

BEGINNING IN 1844, the State of Louisiana began leasing out people convicted of crimes to labor for private individuals and entities.

This convict-lease system was designed as a public–private partnership that would remove the state's financial burden of operating a prison. Before the Civil War, the lease was limited to the

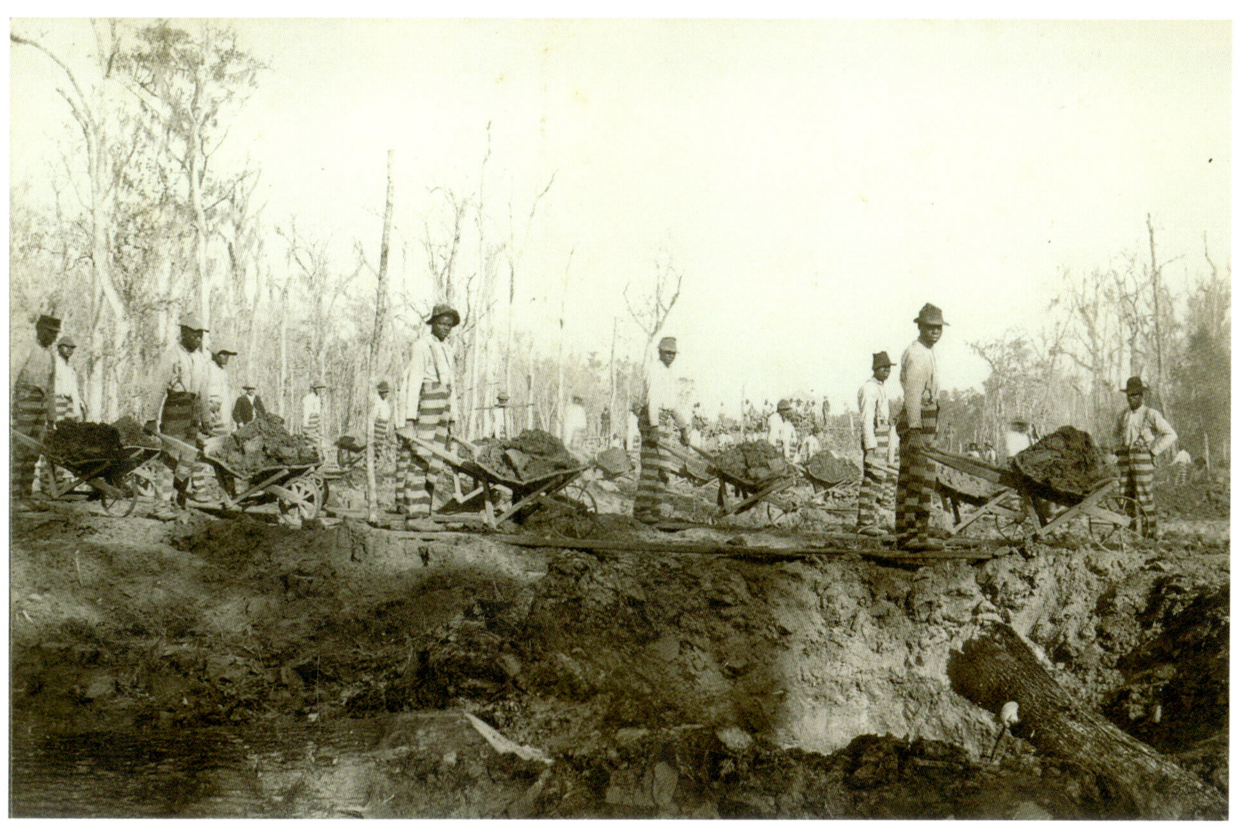

Levee construction, Atchafalaya River; 1900 or 1901; gelatin silver print by Andrew D. Lytle; *courtesy of LSU Libraries, Special Collections, Andrew D. Lytle's Baton Rouge Photograph Collection*

operation of the first Louisiana State Penitentiary, located in Baton Rouge, which opened in 1835 and became known as the Walls for its imposing brick fortifications. Most state prisoners before the Civil War were white, in large part because punishments for people of color were administered directly by enslavers or by police and police jails.

In 1844 Louisiana leased the operation of the Louisiana State Penitentiary in Baton Rouge to James McHatton and William Pratt. McHatton and Pratt used the incarcerated population in their custody as a labor source for financial benefit. To further this plan of exploitation, they outfitted the penitentiary with industrial textile production machinery.

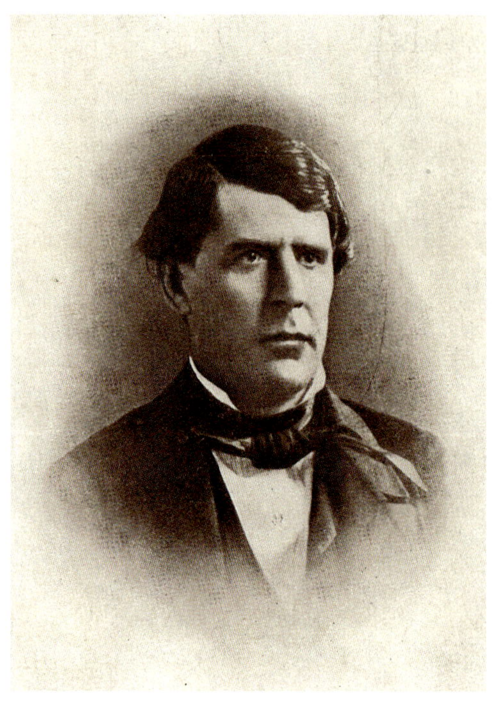

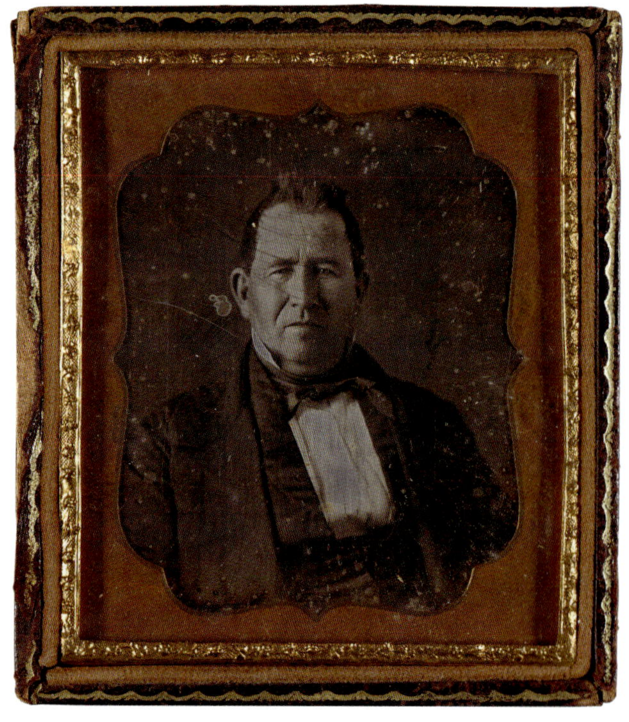

James Alexander McHatton; from *Social Life in Old New Orleans* (New York: D. Appleton and Company, 1912); *HNOC, gift of Ralph M. Pons, 76-960-RL*

William Pratt; between 1845 and 1855; daguerreotype; *HNOC, gift of John Sarradet, 2025.0095*

Following the expiration of the lease in 1849, Pratt ended his partnership in the operation. McHatton continued to operate the penitentiary through the 1850s with a succession of partners. He was able to turn a significant profit in its operation, prompting the state to negotiate for a greater percentage of profit in ensuing contracts. His administration was known to be particularly brutal for incarcerated people.

After the Civil War, the convict-lease system and incarceration by the state replaced slavery as the primary method of controlling Black people and holding them in captivity. The Thirteenth Amendment to the United States Constitution, which abolished most forms of slavery, included an exception for enslaving people convicted of a crime.

Thirteenth Amendment, Section One

Neither slavery nor involuntary servitude, except as a punishment for crime whereof the party shall have been duly convicted, shall exist within the United States, or any place subject to their jurisdiction.

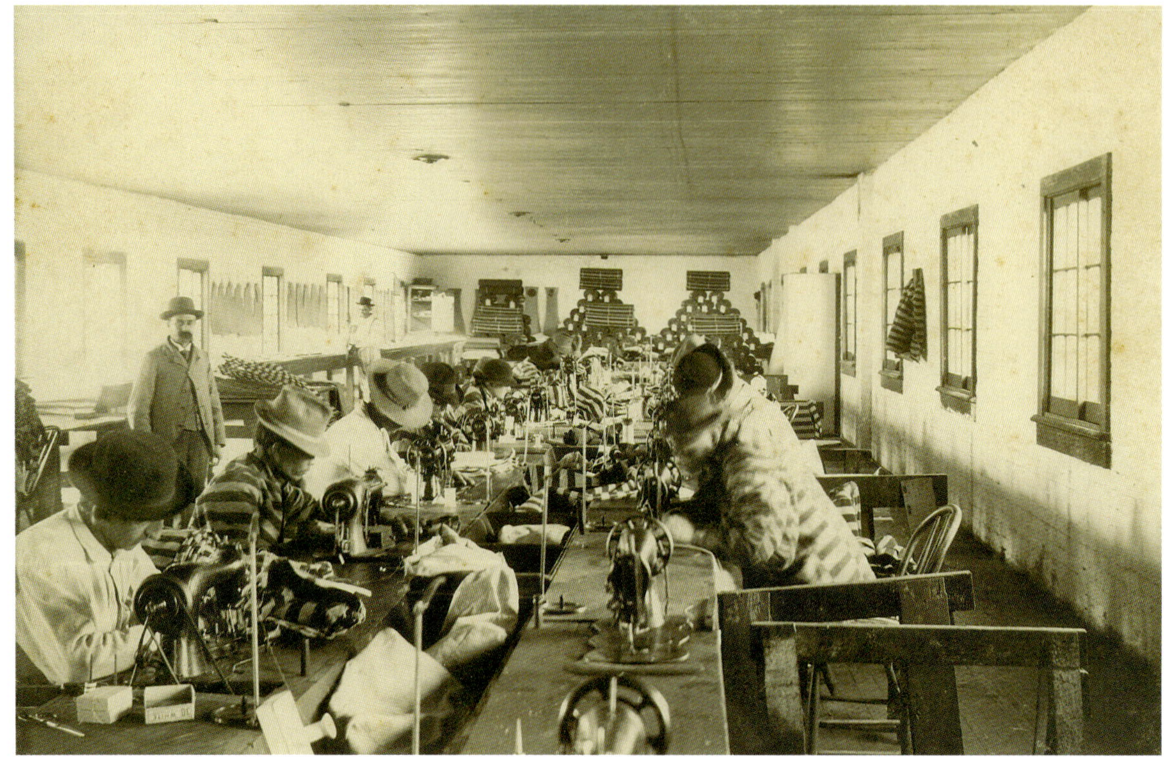

Clothing factory, Louisiana State Penitentiary (the Walls), Baton Rouge; between 1900 and 1901; gelatin silver print by Andrew D. Lytle; *courtesy of LSU Libraries, Special Collections, Andrew D. Lytle's Baton Rouge Photograph Collection*

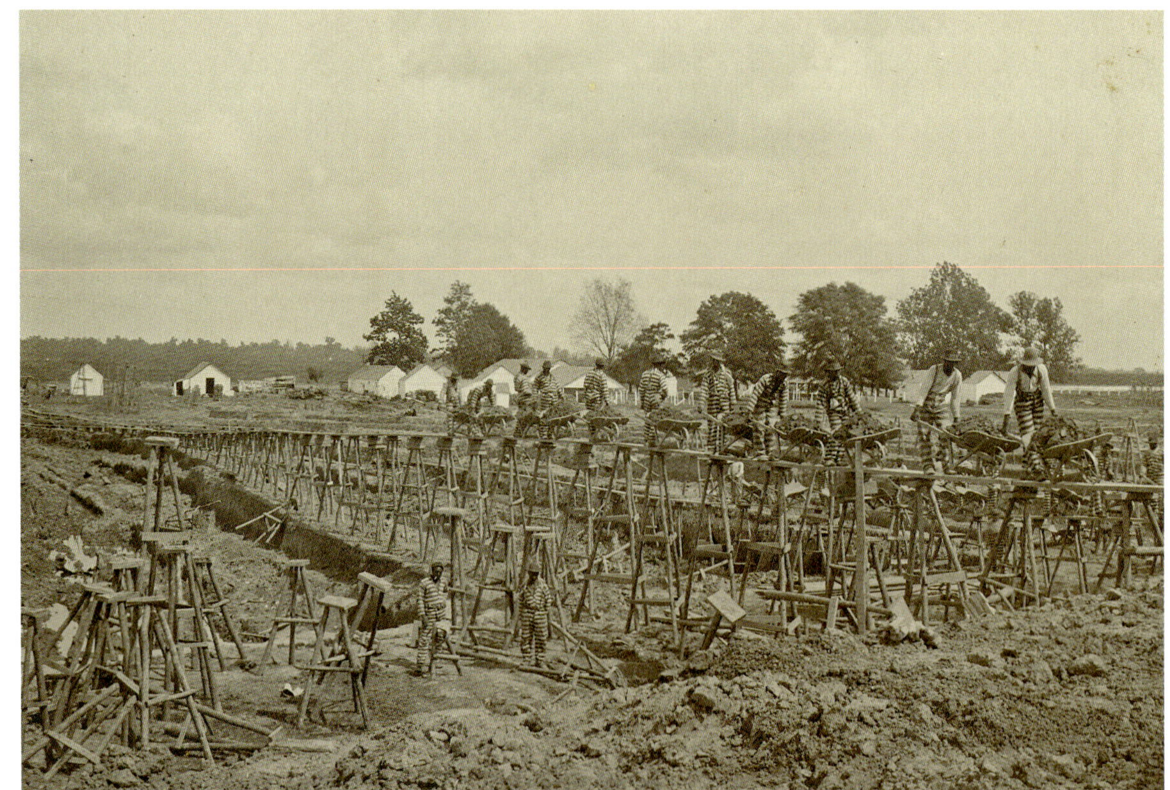

Levee construction near Angola; between 1900 and 1901; gelatin silver print by Andrew D. Lytle; *courtesy of LSU Libraries, Special Collections, Andrew D. Lytle's Baton Rouge Photograph Collection*

"Slavery has never been abolished in these United States of America."

—CURTIS DAVIS, PROMISE OF JUSTICE INITIATIVE INTERVIEW, 2022

Over the subsequent decades, Louisiana legislators made a number of changes that dramatically increased the number of Black people sentenced to state prison. The demographics of the state prison population essentially reversed, from majority white before the Civil War to majority Black after the passage of the Thirteenth Amendment.

THE RISE OF ANGOLA

IN THE 1830S the slave trader Isaac Franklin, one of the largest enslavers of his era, acquired a group of plantations in West Feliciana Parish—Angola, Bellevue, Loango, Lake Killarney, Panola, Monrovia, and Lochlomand—which he and his family operated through the Civil War. In 1880 the properties, which

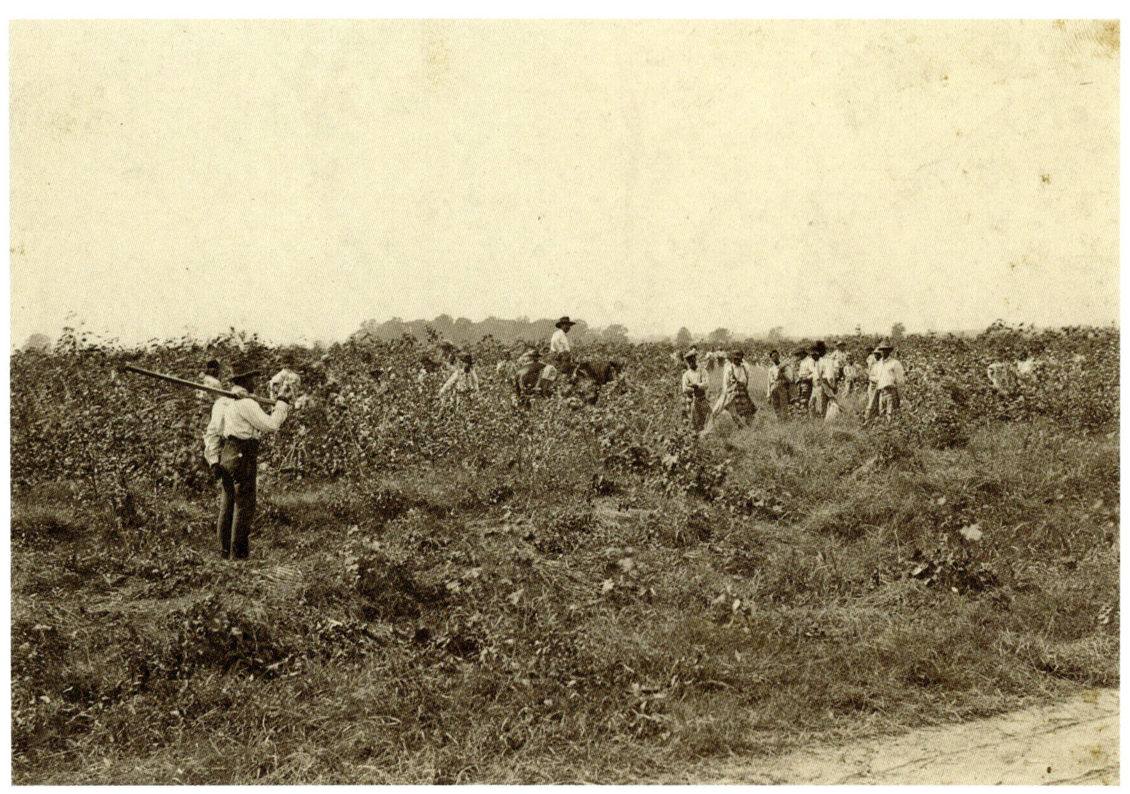

Harvesting cotton, Angola; between 1900 and 1901; gelatin silver print by Andrew D. Lytle; *courtesy of LSU Libraries, Special Collections, Andrew D. Lytle's Baton Rouge Photograph Collection*

totaled over ten thousand acres, were sold to Samuel L. James.

James, a former Confederate officer, had purchased the lease for all of Louisiana's convicted state prisoners in 1870. During the James lease, which lasted through the end of the nineteenth century, the bulk of labor operations shifted from the Walls in Baton Rouge to infrastructure projects and plantation work across the state. While white male prisoners, a relatively small cohort, principally labored indoors in textile and shoe manufacturing at the Walls, the incarcerated Black population was engaged in dangerous outdoor physical labor on James's plantations, on levees, and elsewhere.

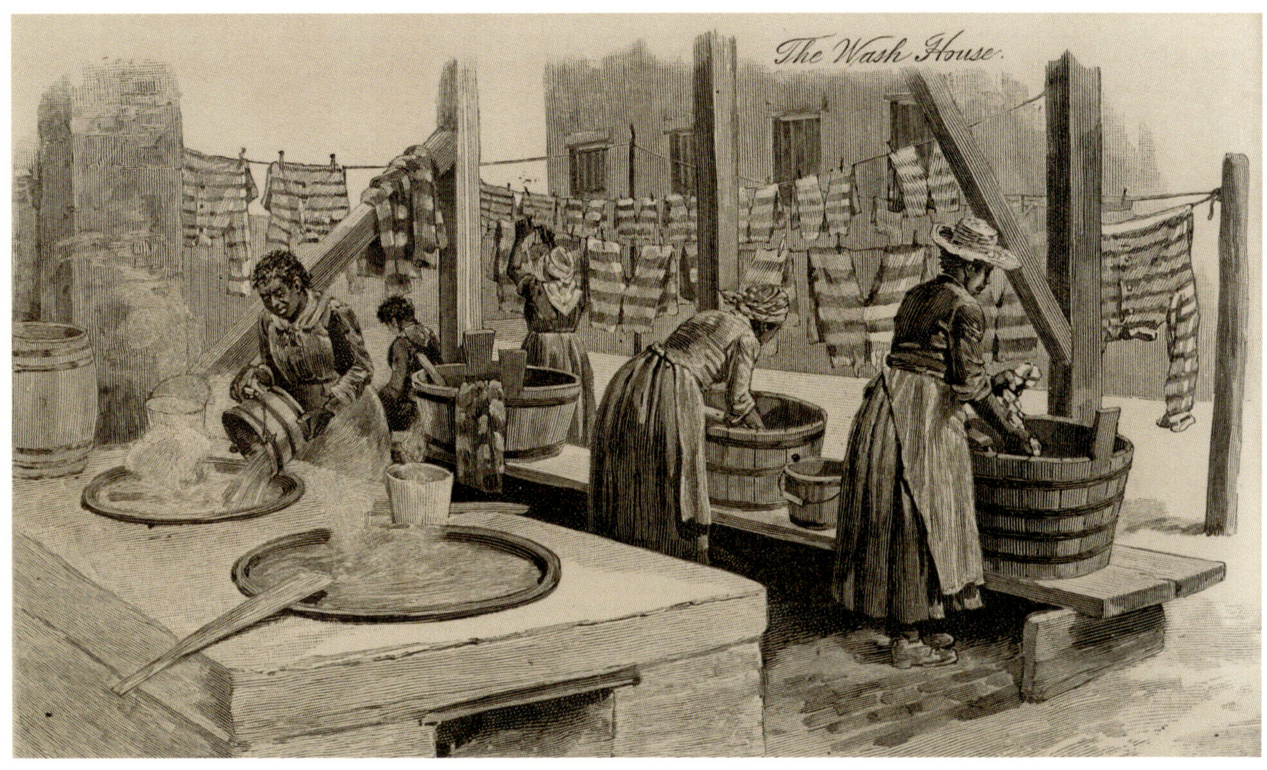

WOMEN UNDER THE CONVICT LEASE

Women incarcerated in Louisiana during the convict-lease era were typically required to work in the laundry or in the fields. In 1878 there were thirty-four women incarcerated in Louisiana, all but one of whom was Black. Of this group, fifteen were subleased to private individuals or entities and the remaining eighteen were held at the Walls in Baton Rouge, laboring "in washing and other such duties," according to a state senate report. In 1881 the female population was relocated by Samuel L. James to Angola.[2]

The Wash House; engraving by John Durkin; from *Harper's Weekly*, August 2, 1890; *HNOC, 79-55-L.2.1*

PROFILES

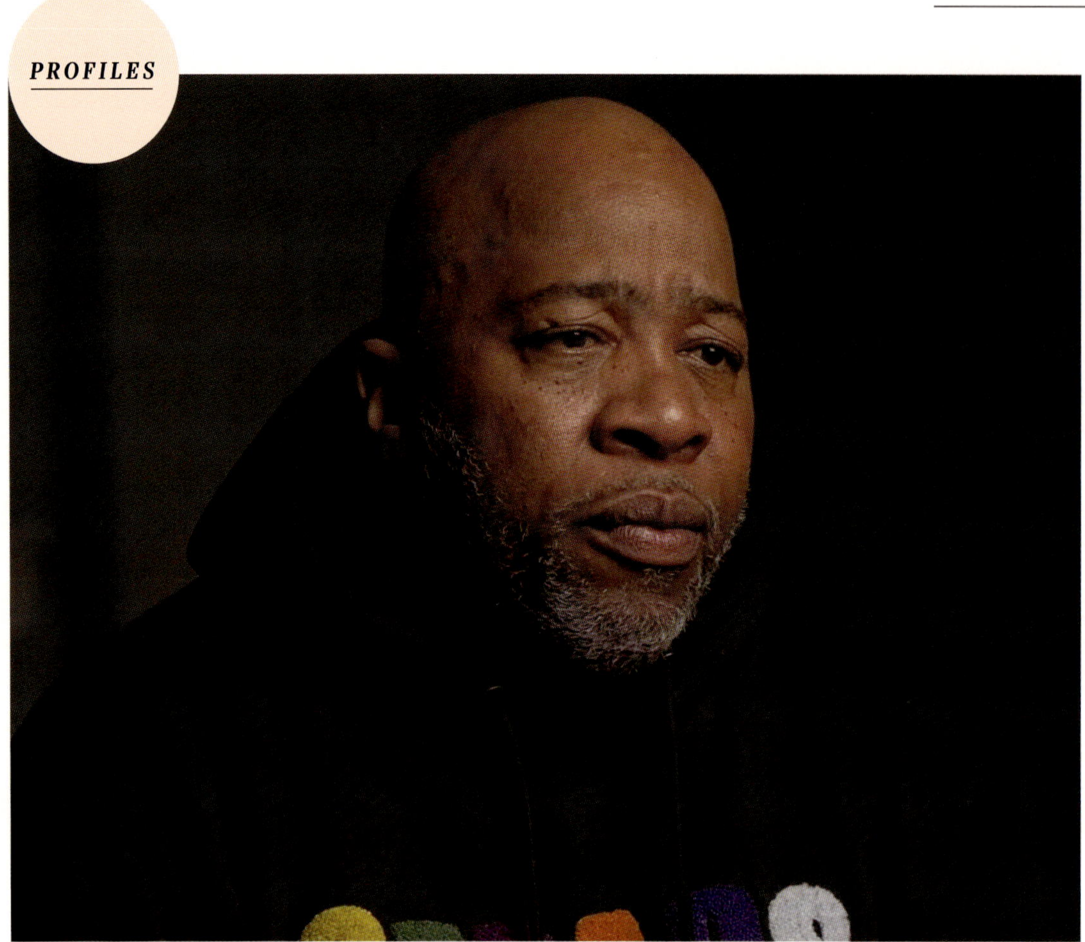

CURTIS DAVIS

"When I went [to Angola] in 1992, I was relegated directly to the field. We picked cotton, fruit products. . . . They have a crawfish farm. They have pecan orchards. They have strawberries they grow there. They have okra, cotton, soybeans, corn for ethanol, and corn for eating. They have over five thousand head of cattle that sell milk. They also sell black Angus cattle for beef processes. Eighteen thousand acres. The same size as Manhattan, New York. . . .

"Slavery has never been abolished in these United States of America. It has been codified into law through the Thirteenth Amendment and the Louisiana Constitution."

This is excerpted from the transcript of an interview produced by the Promise of Justice Initiative, in partnership with Decarcerate Louisiana and Professor Andrea Armstrong at Loyola University New Orleans College of Law for the End Plantation Prisons project. Davis was pardoned and released in 2016 after serving nearly twenty-six years in prison.

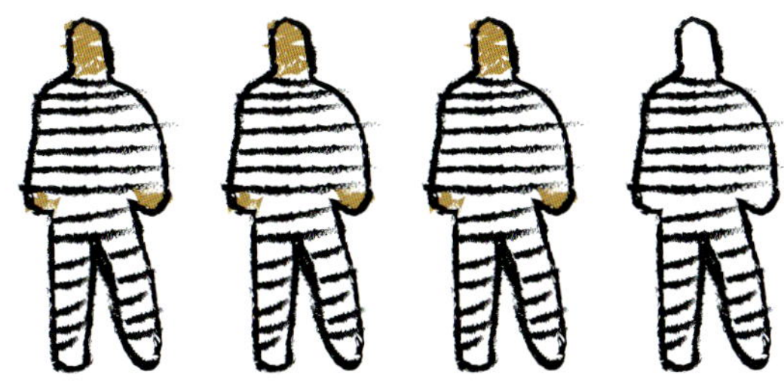

During the James lease, ***about three in four state prisoners were Black.***

An average of 100 prisoners—one out of every seven—died each year under James's oversight.[3]

The same year James purchased his plantations, Louisiana passed a law reducing the requirement for criminal conviction from unanimity to nine of twelve jurors. The state would also update vagrancy laws and introduce multiple misdemeanor provisions. All of these legal changes helped to transform the demographics and increase the size of the state prison population. Over the course of thirty years, James used this captive and predominantly Black workforce to create profit and wealth for himself and his family. Thousands of people died under his oversight.

The state chose not to renew the James lease following its expiration in 1900. In 1901 Louisiana purchased most of the plantations from his estate, which came to be known collectively by a single name: Angola. By 1908, 1,860 people were incarcerated by the State of Louisiana on plantations where cotton, sugarcane, corn, peas, cattle, and hogs were cultivated. Today the site remains in operation as the Louisiana State Penitentiary, a prison farm that has operated continuously with forced labor for nearly two hundred years. In many ways, the conditions experienced by people incarcerated at Angola changed little into the twentieth century.

1 Mancini, *One Dies, Get Another*, 3.

2 Louisiana, *Report of the Senate Committee*, 4.

3 Carleton, *Politics and Punishment*, 46, 89; Mancini, 146; Hair, "Bourbon Democracy," 132; Aiello, *Jim Crow's Last Stand*, 13; Carleton, "Convict Lease System," 25n53.

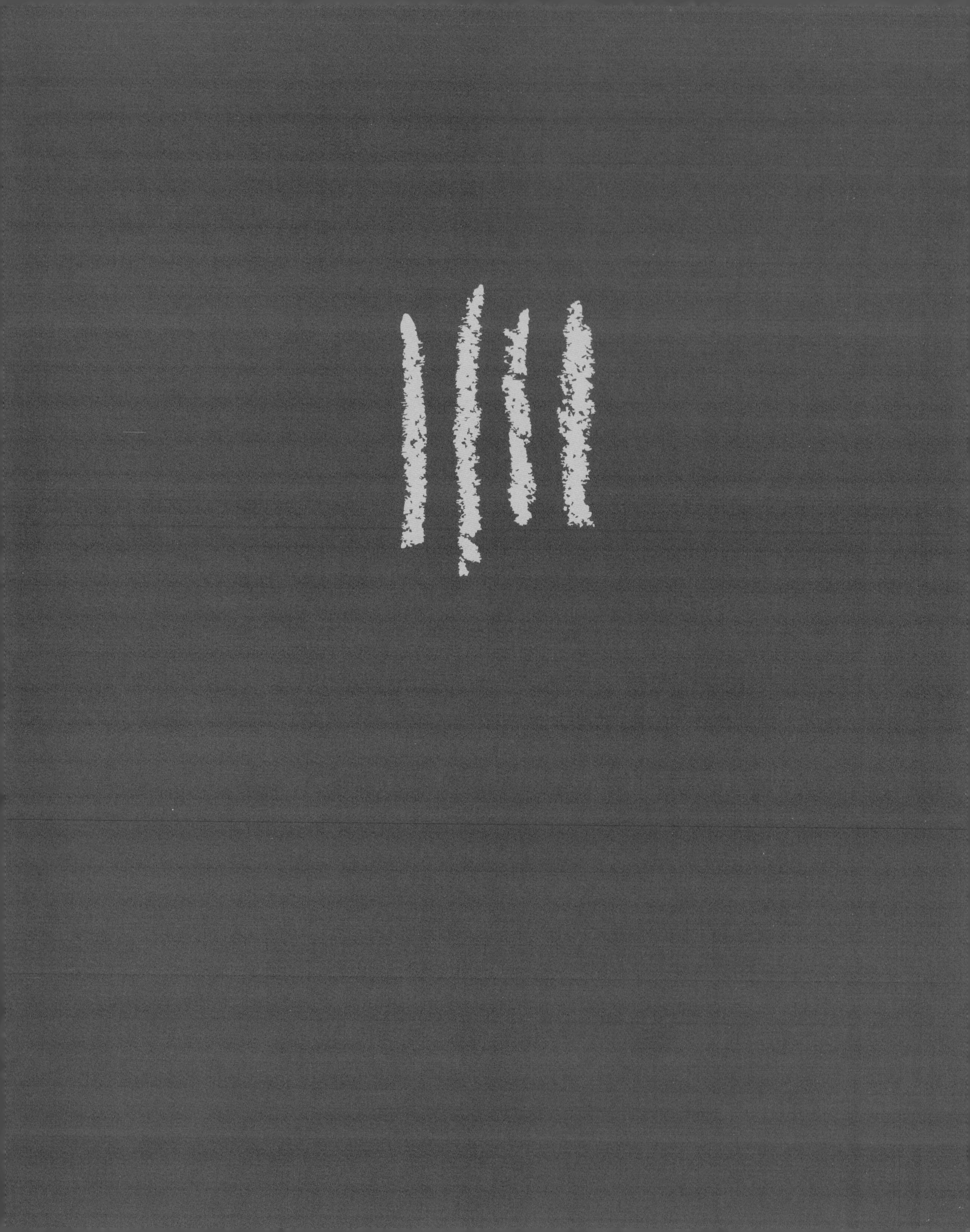

Chapter Four

A BLUEPRINT FOR MASS INCARCERATION

"Our mission was, in the first place, to establish the supremacy of the white race in this State."

—THOMAS J. SEMMES, CHAIRMAN OF THE COMMITTEE ON THE JUDICIARY, 1898 LOUISIANA CONSTITUTIONAL CONVENTION[1]

ANTI-BLACK LAWS and practices established during Louisiana's colonial and early American eras fueled a rapid rise in incarceration in the twentieth century.

At the end of the nineteenth century, a group of white men came together to draft a new state constitution in Louisiana with the express purpose of maintaining white supremacy. The resulting document enshrined Jim Crow racial apartheid into law. The Louisiana Constitution of 1898 helped define how, why, and where people would be incarcerated in the twentieth century, and it acted as a legal bridge between eras, adapting old methods of social control and exploitation for the Jim Crow era and beyond.

Among other things, the constitution maintained the practice of forced

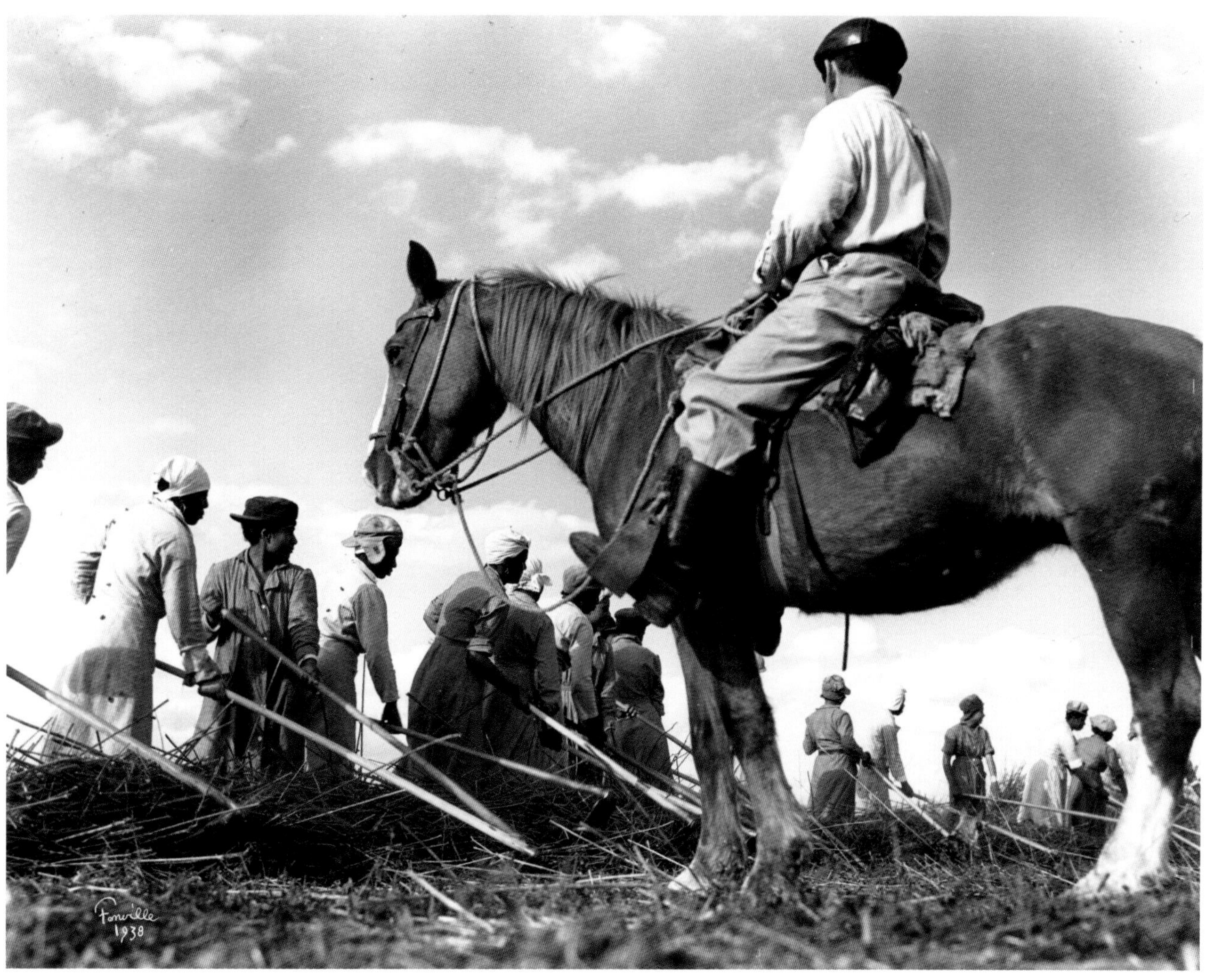

labor and returned all convicted persons to state custody, ending the convict-lease era. By returning convicted persons to state custody and codifying the use of forced labor, the constitution permitted the state to operate the Louisiana State Penitentiary at Angola as a prison farm. To this day, incarcerated people are forced to labor at Angola with antiquated tools in much the same way that enslaved people worked on the site when it was a plantation.

This includes incarcerated women, who were held at Angola from 1881 until 1961, when the state opened the Louisiana Correctional Institute for Women. During their years at Angola, incarcerated Black women usually worked in the fields, as seen in the above photo.

Angola Hoers; 1938; gelatin silver print by Fonville Winans; *HNOC, 2018.0513.9*

Article 116.

The General Assembly shall provide for the selection of competent and intelligent jurors. All cases in which the punishment may not be at hard labor shall, until otherwise provided by law, which shall not be prior to 1904, be tried by the judge without a jury. Cases in which the punishment may be at hard labor shall be tried by a jury of five, all of whom must concur to render a verdict; cases in which the punishment is necessarily at hard labor, by a jury of twelve, nine of whom concurring may render a verdict; cases in which the punishment may be capital, by a jury of twelve, all of whom must concur to render a verdict:

Detail of Article 116 of the 1898 Louisiana State Constitution (emphasis added); photograph by Keely Merritt, HNOC; *courtesy of Louisiana State Archives*

The framers of this constitution also wanted to weaken Black people's influence in criminal trials. To do this, they included a provision (first laid out in an 1880 law) that only nine of twelve jurors must concur to convict someone of a felony. By codifying the use of nonunanimous jury convictions (Article 116), the constitution made it easier to produce guilty pleas and verdicts—particularly from Black defendants. It also effectively nullified the votes of Black jurors. This provision would remain on the books for more than a century.

FORCED LABOR IN THE CITY

NEW ORLEANS CONTINUED to depend on incarcerated labor into the twen-

"This department has to rely upon . . . prisoners to clean public buildings, markets, and squares, not having had any money budgeted for labor."

—NEW ORLEANS COMMISSIONER OF POLICE JOHNATHAN W. MURPHY, 1899

tieth century. Its consolidated jail, renamed the Police Jail in 1881, housed municipal work gangs, which consisted of Black prisoners employed in sanitation and infrastructure development. The city's commissioner of police and public buildings, Johnathan W. Murphy, needed workers so desperately that in 1899 he asked City Court Judge A. M. Aucoin to sentence more people to labor in the Police Jail. He wrote to the judge, "This department has to rely upon . . . prisoners to clean public buildings, markets, and squares, not having had any money budgeted for labor."[2]

In 1901, the city rechristened this facility once again, as the House of Detention (HOD). Officials opened a brand-new HOD three year later at the intersection of Tulane Avenue and Broad Street. The city continued to rely on coerced labor from people incarcerated there into the new century. The location remains home to the city's jail complex, which grew rapidly in the latter half of the twentieth century to accommodate an explosion in incarceration rates.

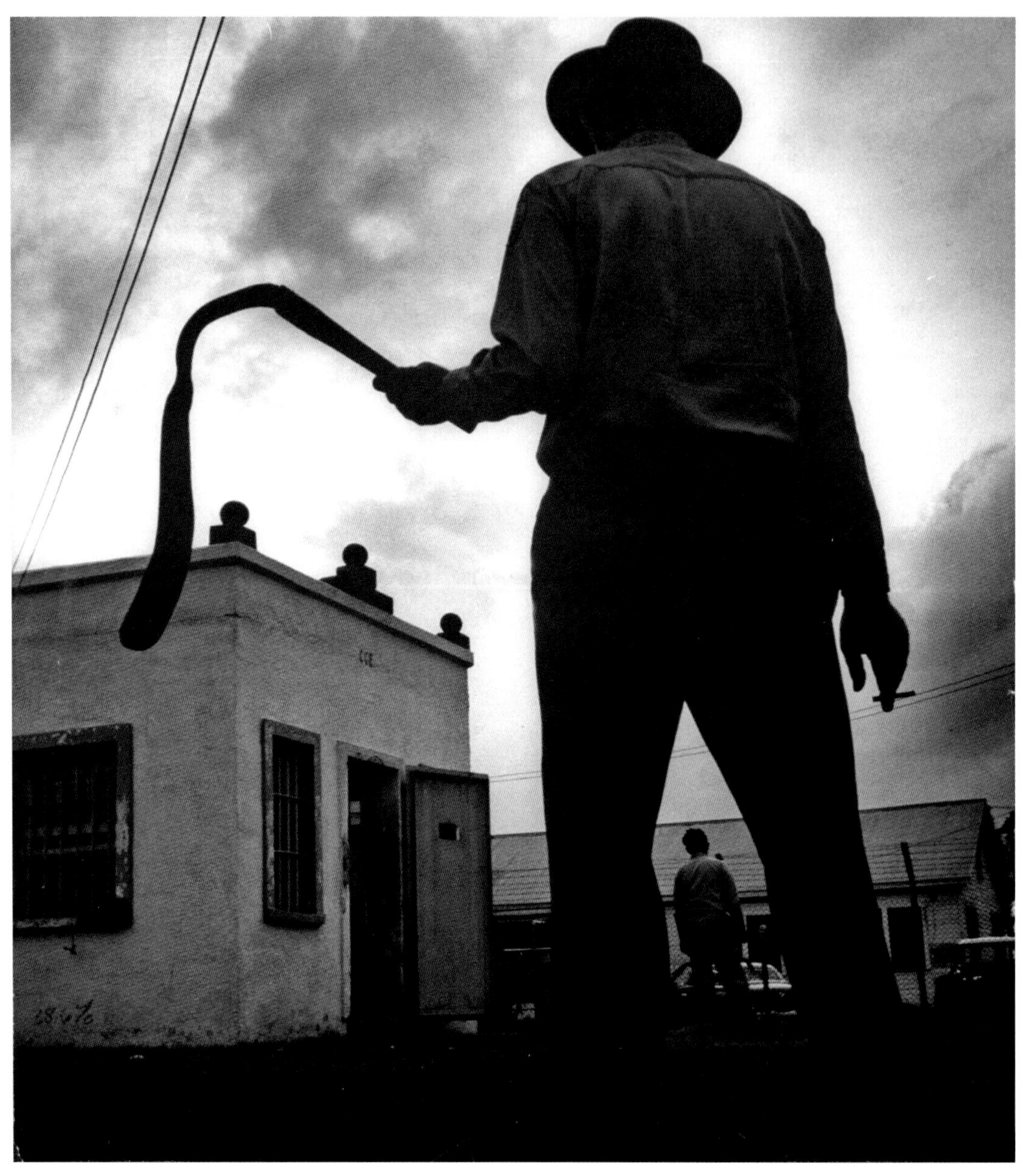

Prison guard holding bullwhip; 1955; photograph by Robert W. Kelley; *courtesy of the LIFE Picture Collection*

ANGOLA ON EDGE

INTO THE TWENTIETH CENTURY, the dangerous and inhumane conditions at the racially segregated Louisiana State Penitentiary at Angola remained similar to those found on the site when it was a slave plantation in the nineteenth century. Beginning in the Great Depression, a raft of cost-cutting measures made matters worse, so much so that in 1951 thirty-seven prisoners slashed their Achilles tendons with razors in protest. The act garnered national attention, including a 1955 photo essay in *Life* magazine.[3]

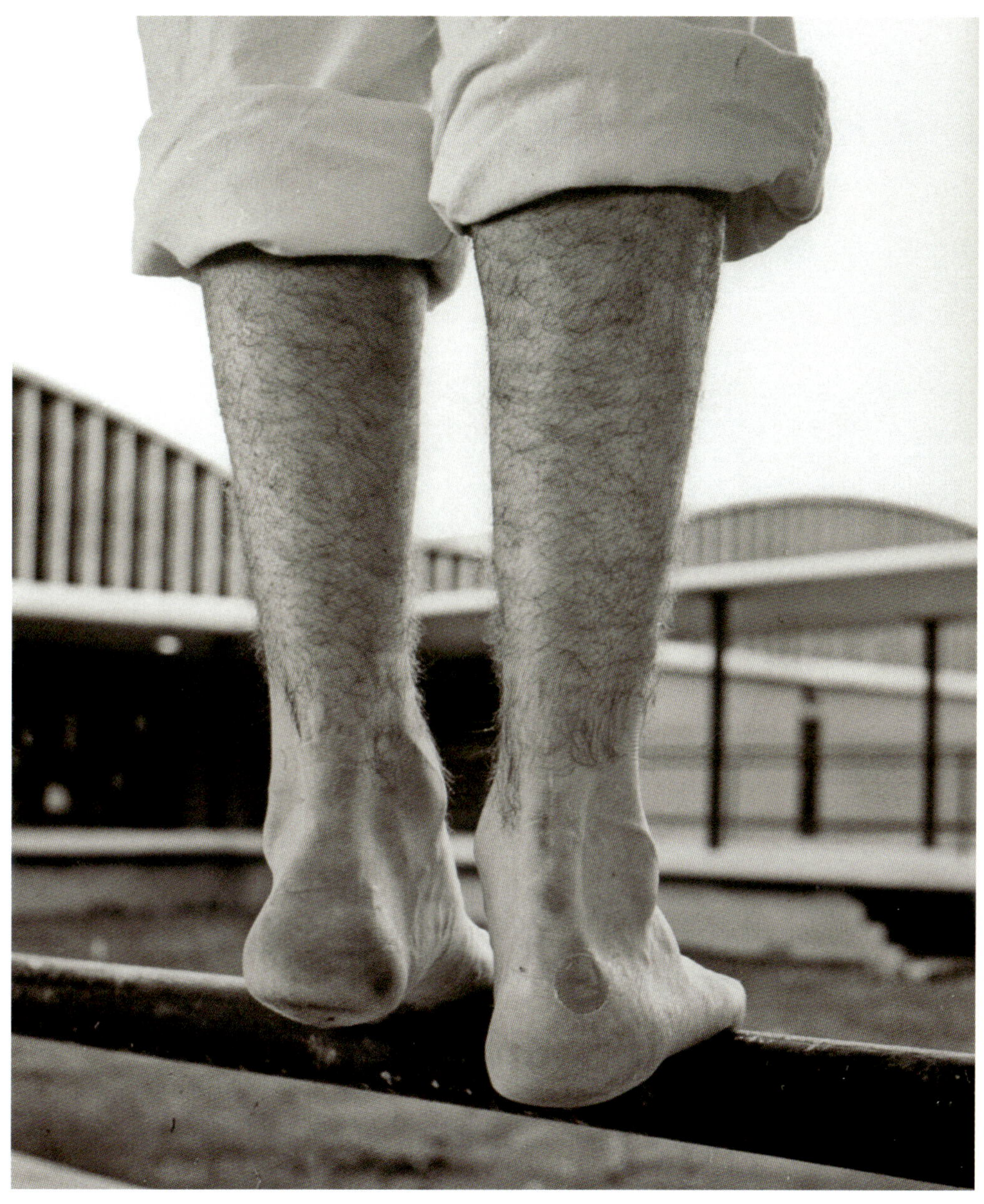

Scarred heels of prisoner at Angola; 1955; photograph by Robert W. Kelley; *courtesy of the LIFE Picture Collection*

A series of court cases starting in the early 1970s found that the conditions at Angola violated the Eighth Amendment to the US Constitution barring cruel and unusual punishment. Judge E. Gordon West of the US Middle District Court wrote that these conditions would "shock the conscience of any right-thinking person."

Since the 1970s, state and local departments overseeing prisons and jails in Louisiana have repeatedly been subjected to federal oversight because of constitutionally inadequate treatment of incarcerated people.[4]

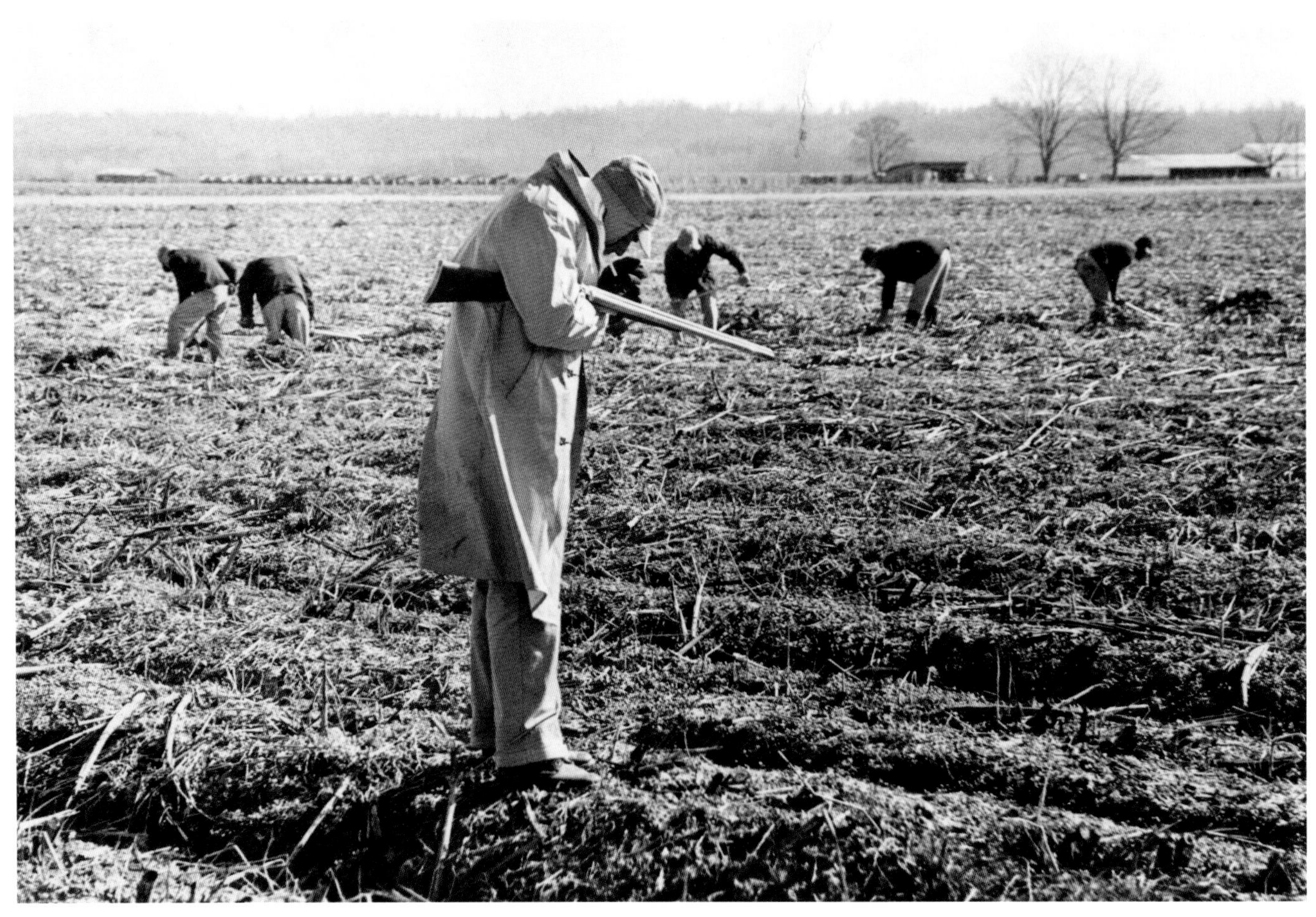

Incarcerated laborers work the fields at Angola; 1965; gelatin silver print by Leonard Freed; *HNOC, 2021.0145.2*

"TOUGH ON CRIME"

IN THE 1970s, legislators, prosecutors, and judges initiated a national tough-on-crime movement that sent more people to prison for longer terms than ever before. In Louisiana, a series of new laws, in concert with the

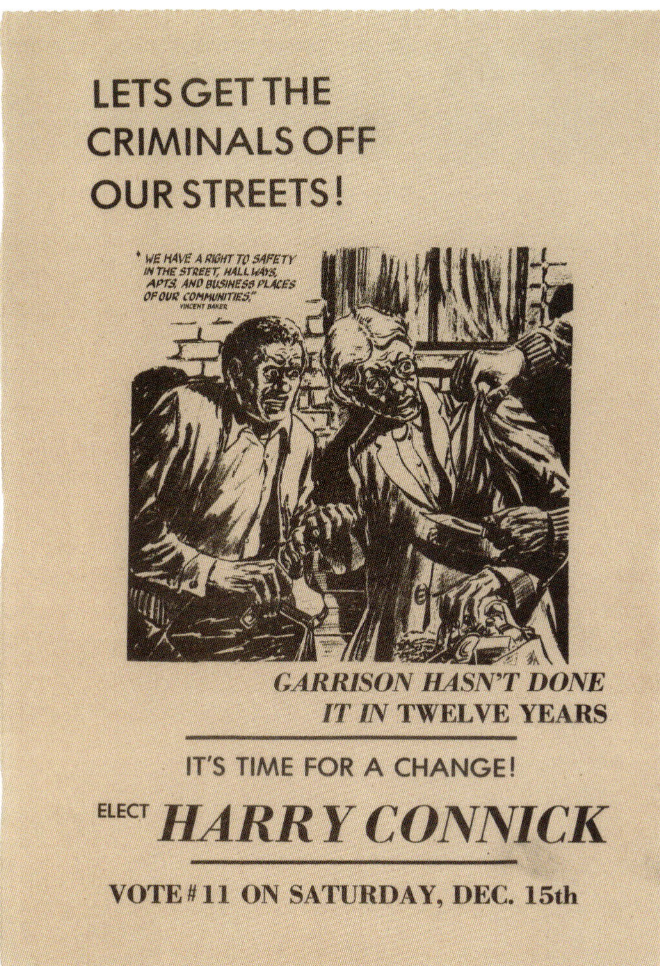

Harry Connick is back

And this time He's going to win.

Four years ago Harry Connick ran for District Attorney against one of the most powerful politicians ever to occupy that office.

Harry Connick ran because he saw the deterioration of justice in the District Attorney's offices—because he saw that if this situation continued, crime would continue to grow in New Orleans.

Even without widespread help, with limited funds, he ran a great race and narrowly lost. And as he predicted, the office of District Attorney has continued to break down and crime has continued to increase.

Harry Connick ran four years ago when others would not. He ran because he saw something wrong and dedicated himself to making it right.

Harry Connick is back in the race and this time he's going to win. He's supported by individuals and organized groups in every section of this city, by those people who now know that we will never do anything about our situation without a trained, capable prosecutor in this important office.

Most of all, Harry Connick is going to win because he is the choice of the public that is demanding change in this office, who have had enough of fear and assaults and robberies and murders, who know that the present District Attorney's office is leaderless, wandering along without direction, without any feeling of responsibility to the people of New Orleans.

The time for change is here.

Twelve years ago we could walk our streets. Today you do so with fear, no matter where you live. In some neighborhoods you cannot relax in the porch swing or just sit on the steps like people in New Orleans have always done. In these twelve years we've seen our city go from one of the most pleasant cities in the country to one where fear exists in every neighborhood . . . and all you hear is that New Orleans isn't what it used to be.

Twelve years ago this administration came to office.

You hear people say—what can one man do about it? How can anyone help our situation? That's what the District Attorney's office would like you to believe, to think that you are helpless, that you can't do anything, because there are things that can be done . . . and aren't being done.

You aren't helpless.

You can fight back.

Harry Connick is trained and experienced in the courtroom. He knows the meaning of swift and sure justice. More than that he is familiar with the ways of the criminal and the causes of crime. As a family man he has felt that fear of crime as much as any of us. That's why he's fighting for a chance to help clean up New Orleans.

Harry is willing to fight for us.

Let's fight for him.

Vote No. 11, Harry Connick for District Attorney, and let everyone who would transgress against the public welfare know . . . that for the first time in 12 years there's a District Attorney who means business in the City of New Orleans.

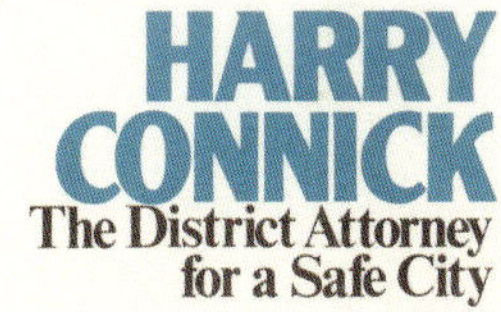

The District Attorney
for a Safe City
#11

3

Connick Campaign Headquarters, 401 Carondelet St., phone 522-5353.

nonunanimous jury provision of the 1898 Constitution, caused incarceration rates in the state to skyrocket. Harry Connick Sr., who served as the New Orleans district attorney from 1973 to 2003, was a powerful force in this movement.

Connick's political ads emphasized his influence in the state legislature. The acts displayed on the following pages were listed in his campaign literature from 1996 and represent a sampling of the legislation he helped get passed at the Louisiana State Capitol.

Harry Connick Sr. campaign fliers; 1973 and 1996; *HNOC, gift of Harry Connick Sr., 2017.0266.301–.302; MSS 857*

1975 Act 337 Allows fifteen- and sixteen-year-olds to be tried as adults for crimes where the penalty is life. ***1975*** *Act 478 Prohibits good time for certain habitual offenders.* ***1977*** *Act 631 Increases the penalty for distribution of Schedule I narcotics.* ***1977*** *Act 632 Increases the penalty for attempt or conspiracy to distribute Schedule I narcotics.* ***1977*** *Act 633 Prohibits awarding of good time to persons sentenced as habitual offenders.* ***1977*** *Act 665 Reduces the maximum monthly award of good time allowed to inmates.* ***1978*** *Act 460 Provides for the transfer of juveniles charged with certain crimes from juvenile court to district court.* ***1979*** *Act 199 Eases certification requirements for proof of out-of-state convictions under the multiple offender statute.* ***1979*** *Act 801 Constitutional amendment to allow courts to treat juveniles who commit certain enumerated crimes as adults.* ***1980*** *Act 311 Prohibits second offenders convicted of distribution, possession with intent to distribute, or manufacture from receiving suspended sentence by participation in a drug rehabilitation program.* ***1982*** *Act 602 Provides for a mandatory minimum penalty of four years at hard labor without benefit of parole, probation, or suspension of sentence relative to distribution and possession with intent to distribute pentazocine.* ***1982*** *Act 703 Redefines crime against nature to include solicitation for unnatural carnal copulation for compensation.* ***1983*** *Act 533 Creates crime of first-degree robbery where victim is led to believe the robber is armed with a dangerous weapon.* ***1984*** *Act 926 Adds life imprisonment crimes to those not having a time limitation for institution of prosecution.* ***1987*** *Act 774 Requires sentences under the Habitual Offender law* *be without benefit of probation or suspension of sentence.* **1989** *Act 171 Provides mandatory prison terms for offenders convicted of violating any felony provision of the Uniform Controlled Dangerous Substances Law within one thousand feet of a school or while on a school bus.* **1991** *Acts 99 and 100 Repeal provisions authorizing the reduction or suspension of certain sentences imposed under the Uniform Controlled Dangerous Substances Act.* **1991** *Act 406 Amends provision allowing court to impose community service in lieu of imposition of sentence.* **1994** *Act 23 Provides for the use of prior juvenile adjudications of felony-grade delinquent acts based upon certain drug violations or the commission of certain crimes of violence.* **1994** *Act 100 Prohibits suspension of sentence for a second conviction of a crime of violence and drug offenses punishable by a term of imprisonment for more than five years.* **1994** *Act 150 Removes good-time provisions for prisoners convicted a second time of crimes of violence.* **1995** *Act 930 Provides for penalty without benefit of parole, probation, or suspension of sentence for narcotics offenses committed with weapons.* **1995** *Act 987 Increases to ten years the minimum penalty for the crime of possession of firearms by a felon.* **1995** *Act 988 Sets minimum penalty of ten years for conviction of attempt of a crime punishable by death or life imprisonment.* **1995** *Act 990 Denies probation to all defendants convicted of crimes of violence as defined in R.S. 14:2 (13).* **1995** *Act 1223 Adds illegal use of firearms to definition of crimes of violence.* **1995** *Act 1251 Repeals and amends various statutes pertaining to expungement of criminal convictions to allow identification of individuals with criminal histories.*

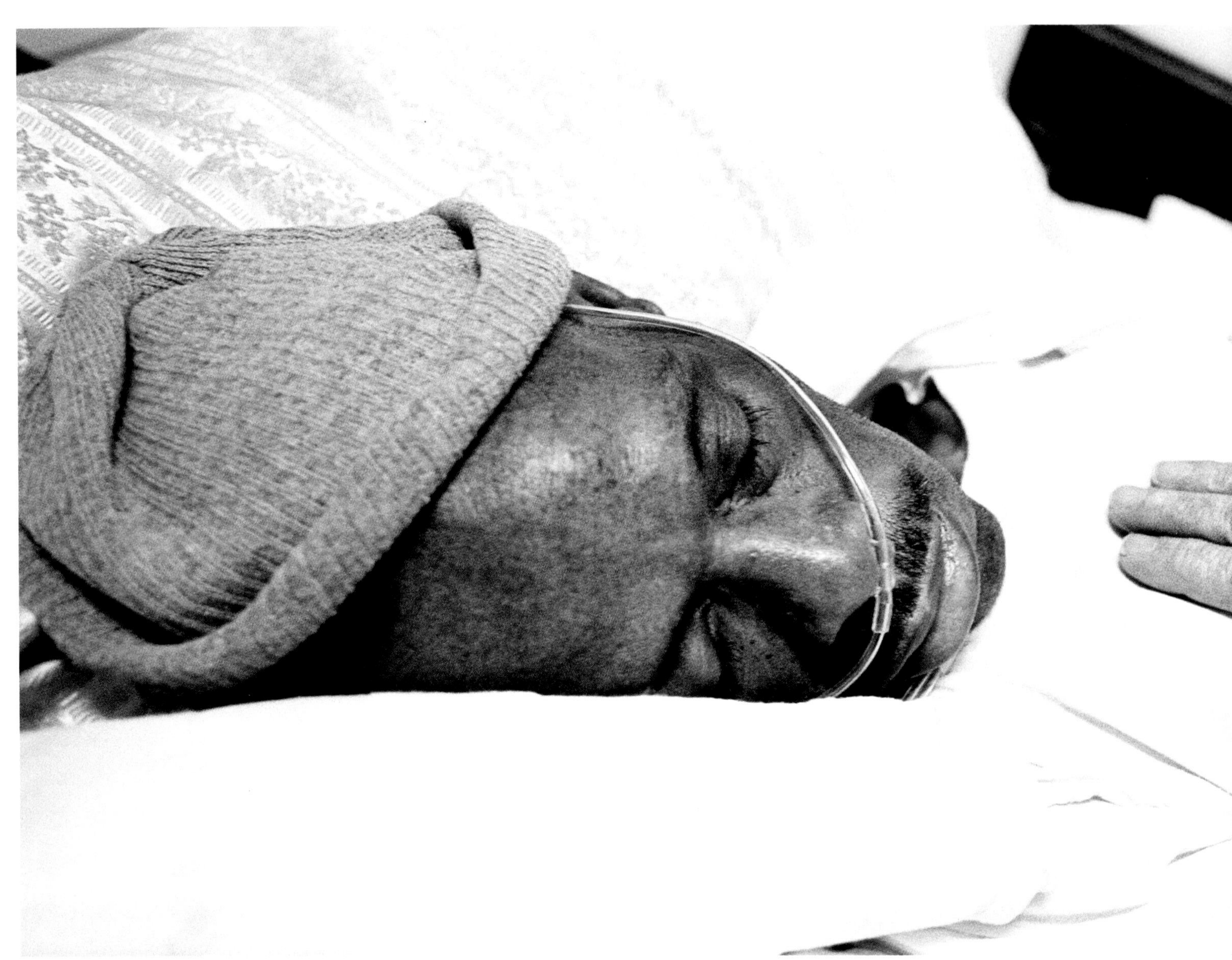

LIFE WITHOUT PAROLE

PRIOR TO 1972, people serving life sentences in Louisiana were eligible for parole after ten years and six months. By 1979, state legislators had abolished parole for these people. At the same time, the state increased the number of offenses

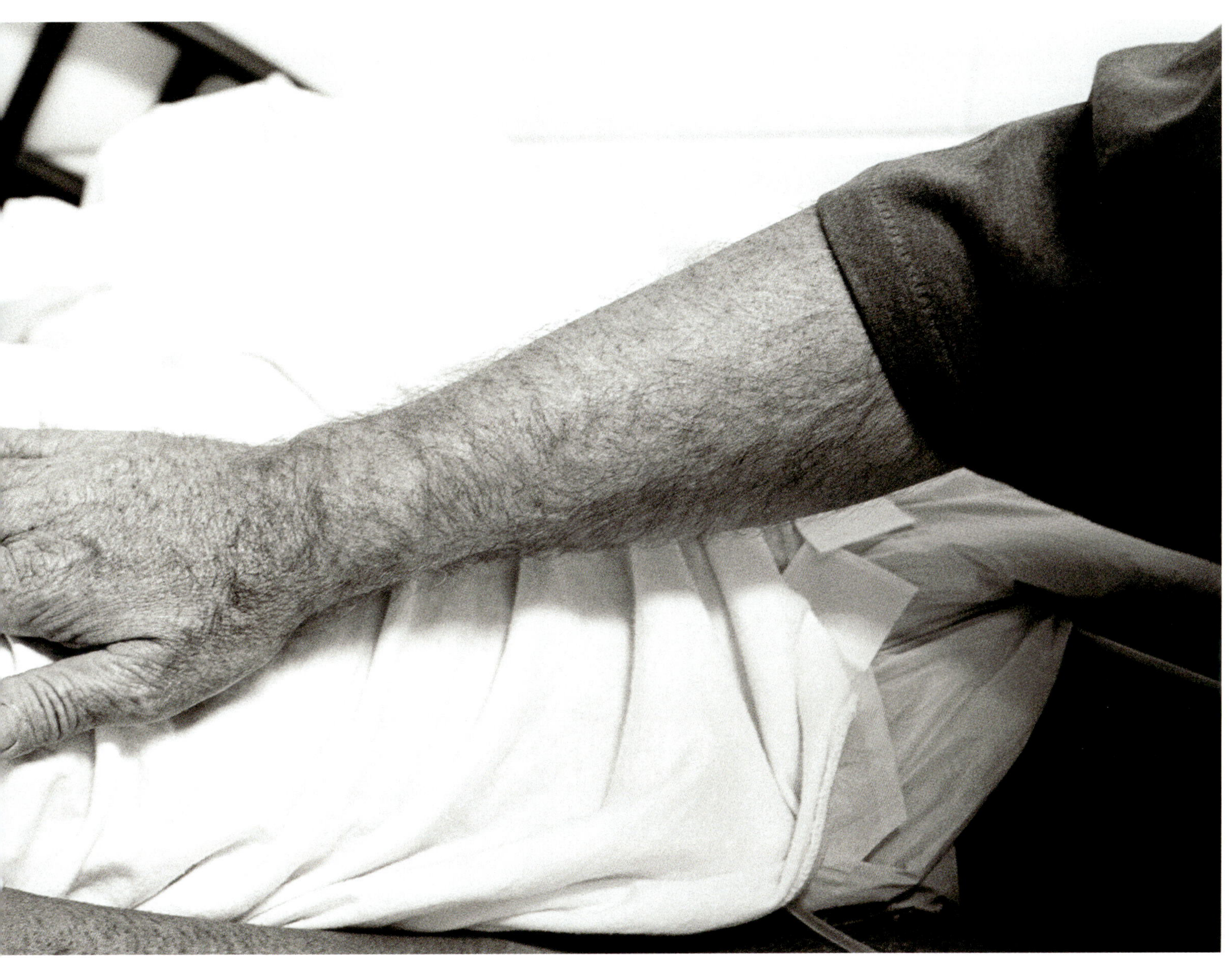

mandating life sentences and continued to convict people with nonunanimous jury decisions. A life sentence means death behind bars in Louisiana.

Due to these "tough on crime" laws championed by Connick and others, more people are serving life sentences for nonviolent crimes in Louisiana than anywhere in the US.[5] This has had a dramatic effect on the demographics of the state prison population. Black people make up a larger proportion of the life-sentence population today than before the abolition of slavery.

George Checks Jimmie's Breathing; 2008; pigment print by Lori Waselchuk; *HNOC, gift of Lori Waselchuk, 2016.0298.3*

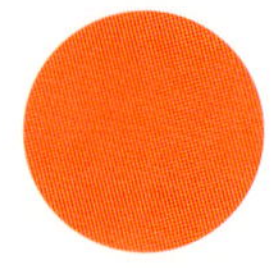

1858

63 percent of people serving life sentences in Louisiana were Black

49 percent of the state population was Black in 1860

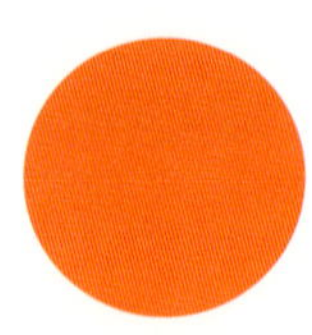

2024

73 percent of people serving life sentences in Louisiana were Black

33 percent of the state's population was Black in 2024

1972

193 people serving life sentences in Louisiana

2024

4,170 people serving life sentences in Louisiana[6]

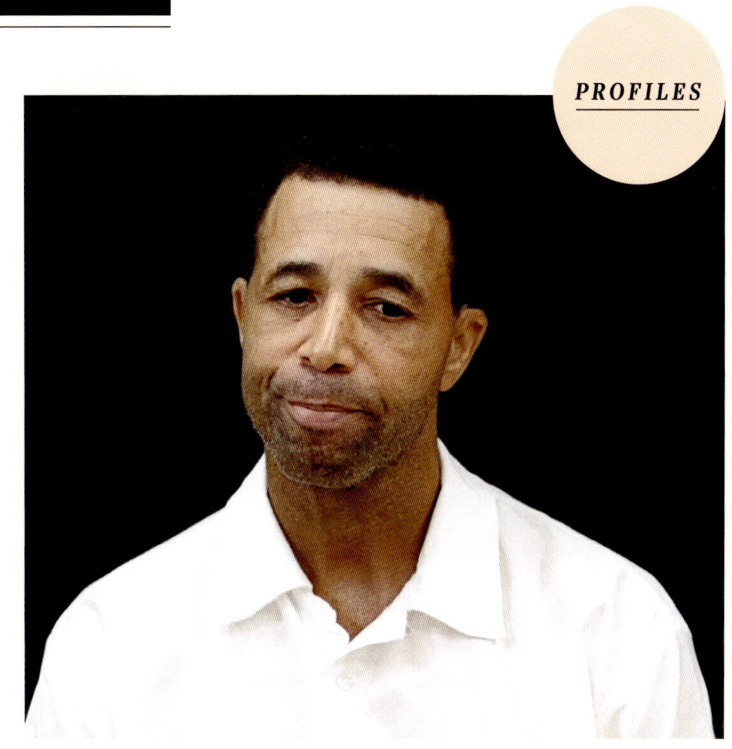

PROFILES

ANTHONY HINGLE JR.

"I was weak in my knees, just hearing the man say 'guilty.' I was actually—I think I probably even buckled a little bit. But I couldn't have thought life meant life because I never felt like I was going to be here the rest of my life. I always felt like, 'I'm not going to die in a penitentiary.' . . . And I think that's what helped me in the very beginning, but I think after being here a while, started associating with other inmates, older guys, I went to hearing it from them, you know, life means life. . . .

"That's the reality of a life sentence. This is what the state wants from you. They want you to grow old, lose your health, sit in one of these beds, till they going to put you in hospice."

This is excerpted from the transcript of an interview conducted by the Visiting Room Project at the Louisiana State Penitentiary in 2017. Hingle's conviction was amended and he was released in 2021 after serving thirty-two years at Angola. He served as a member of the Captive State *exhibition's advisory board.*

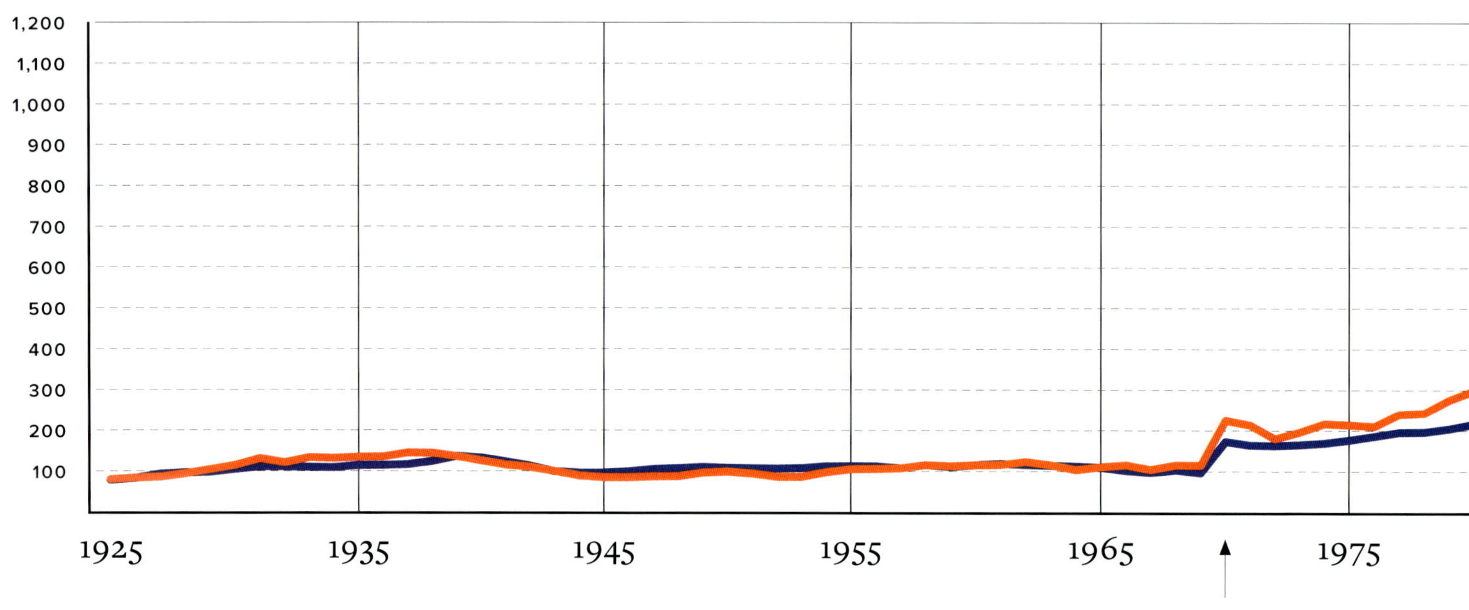
1,200
1,100
1,000
900
800
700
600
500
400
300
200
100
1925
1935
1945
1955
1965
1975
Prior to 1970 jail population data was not regularly collected. This chart combines jail and prison populations beginning in that year.

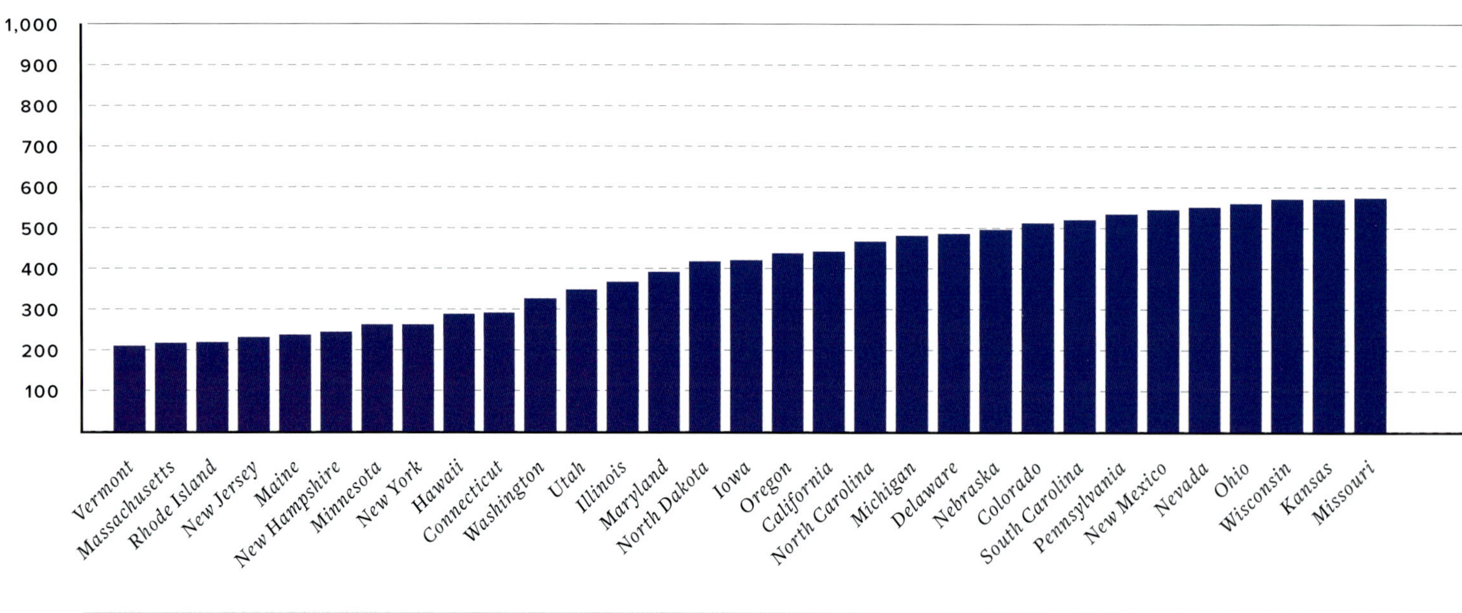
1,000
900
800
700
600
500
400
300
200
100
Vermont
Massachusetts
Rhode Island
New Jersey
Maine
New Hampshire
Minnesota
New York
Hawaii
Connecticut
Washington
Utah
Illinois
Maryland
North Dakota
Iowa
Oregon
California
North Carolina
Michigan
Delaware
Nebraska
Colorado
South Carolina
Pennsylvania
New Mexico
Nevada
Ohio
Wisconsin
Kansas
Missouri

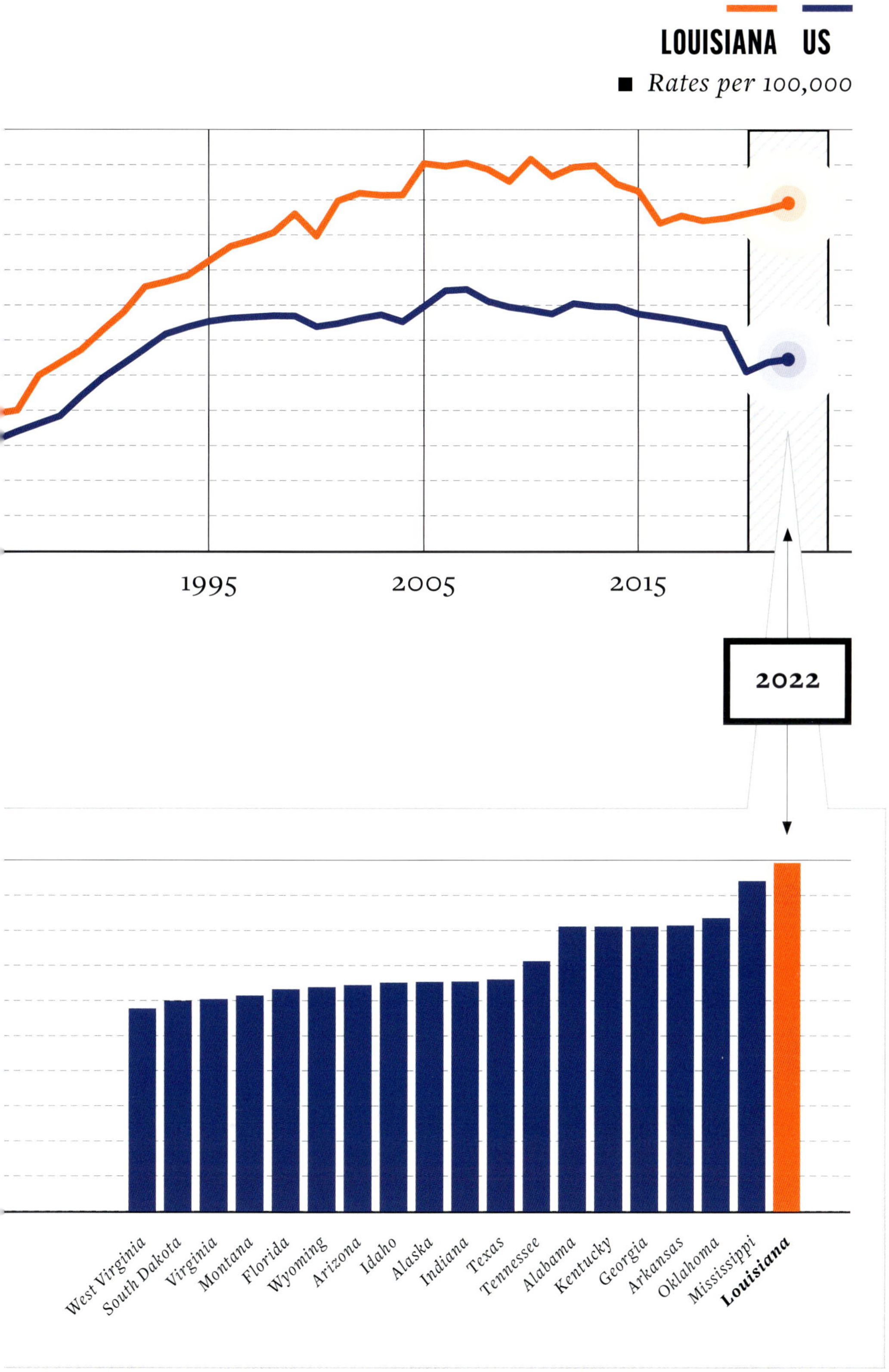

LOUISIANA US

■ *Rates per 100,000*

1995 2005 2015

2022

West Virginia South Dakota Virginia Montana Florida Wyoming Arizona Idaho Alaska Indiana Texas Tennessee Alabama Kentucky Georgia Arkansas Oklahoma Mississippi **Louisiana**

THE RISE OF MASS INCARCERATION

IN THE WAKE of "tough on crime" laws, incarceration rates across the United States rose dramatically in the last decades of the twentieth century and into the twenty-first century. They peaked around 2007 both nationally and in Louisiana, but rates have begun creeping back up in recent years.[7]

In a nation that incarcerates at higher rates than almost anywhere else in the world, Louisiana has managed to consistently outpace the other 49 states.[8] It has led the US in incarceration rates for decades, locking people up at unprecedented levels that disproportionately affect Black people.

1 Louisiana, *Proceedings of the Constitutional Convention*, 375.

2 Bardes, "Mass Incarceration," 410–14.

3 Hallinan, *Going Up the River*, 23.

4 *Hayes Williams et al. v. Edwin Edwards, Governor of the State of Louisiana, et al.*, 547 F.2d 1206 (5th Cir. 1977), Justia.

5 Turner, *A Living Death*, 2.

6 Bardes, "Mass Incarceration," 134; US Census Bureau, "State of Louisiana Table No. 2—Population by Color and Condition," 1860 US Census; US Census Bureau, Louisiana state profile, data.census.gov; Louisiana Department of Public Safety and Corrections, "Demographic Dashboard for Website," update from November 30, 2024, https://doc.louisiana.gov/demographic-dashboard/.

7 Incarceration rates were calculated by dividing the combined prison and jail population for a given year by the corresponding national or state population and multiplying by 100,000. US incarceration rates in this graphic exclude Louisiana for a more accurate comparison. Following the example of Prison Policy Initiative analysts, where data was available, individuals held in jails for federal or state agencies were subtracted from total jail populations to avoid double-counting individuals already enumerated in state prison custody reports. Sources: Langan et al., *Historical Statistics*, 5–15; Bowie, *Prisoners 1925–81*, 1–4; Louisiana Department of Public Safety and Corrections, *Briefing Book*, 1–9; Sawyer and Wagner, *Mass Incarceration*; Zeng and Minton, *Census of Jails*, 7–8, 13–14, 28–29; Carson and Kluckow, *Prisoners in 2022*, 7–8, 26–27; Carson, *Prisoners in 2021*, 6–9, 28–29; Carson, *Prisoners in 2019*, 3–5, 26–27; Carson, *Prisoners in 2016*, 3–4, 22; Carson and Sabol, *Prisoners in 2011*, 2–6, 32; West and Sabol, *Prisoners in 2007*, 1–6, 24; Harrison and Beck, *Prisoners in 2003*, 2–6; Beck, *Prisoners in 1999*, 1–9; Gilliard and Allen, *Prisoners in 1997*, 1–3; Greenfeld, *Prisoners in 1989*, 1–2; Prison Policy Initiative, "Appendix Table 5, Jail and Prison Incarceration Populations by State, 1978-2022," 2024, https://www.prisonpolicy.org/reports/jails2024_table5.html; National Criminal Justice Information and Statistics Service, *National Jail Census, 1970*, 9; National Criminal Justice Information and Statistics Service, *The Nation's Jails*, 23–24. All national and state population data from the US Census Bureau. Jail populations for 1971 and 1973–77 calculated based on a linear trajectory between other years with data.

8 Widra, *States of Incarceration*, Appendix 1; Zeng and Minton, *Census of Jails*, 13; Carson and Kluckow, *Prisoners in 2022*, 7–8, 26–27. In order to put state rates in context with national rates, which include years where less comprehensive data is available, rates displayed on pages 66 and 67 are based solely on people held in prisons and jails and exclude about 15 percent of the total incarcerated population, which includes people held in juvenile detention centers, Immigration and Customs Enforcement detention centers, and other places. As a result, these rates slightly underestimate total incarceration. The rates for Louisiana and the US shown on page 11 are more comprehensive.

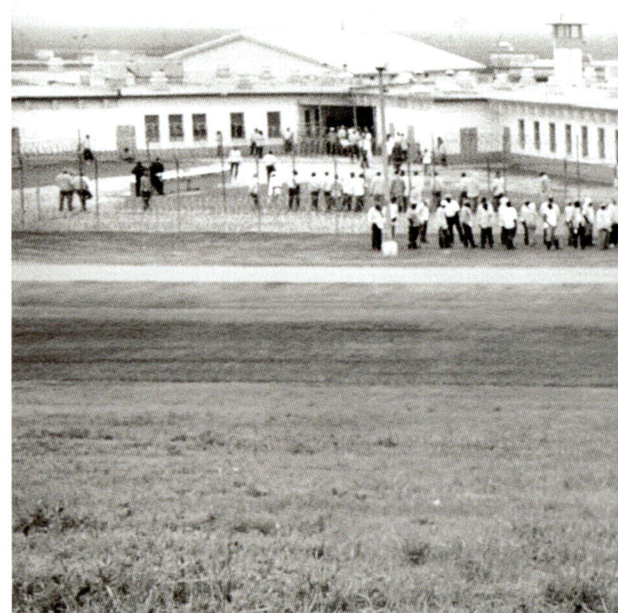

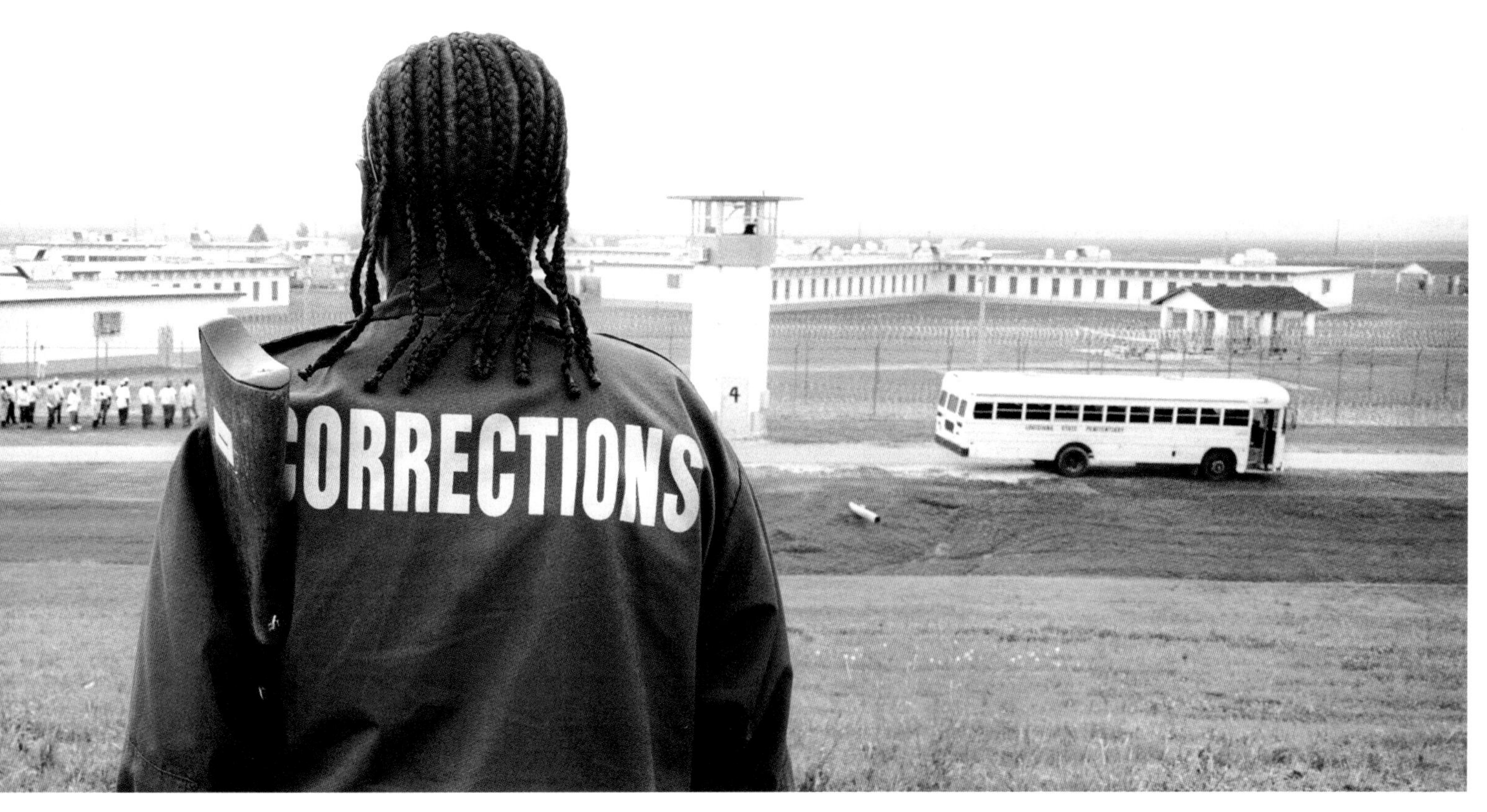

Prison Guard Watches from the Levee; 2007; pigment print by Lori Waselchuk; *HNOC, 2016.0299.1*

Chapter Five

BREAKING POINTS

"The more space we build, the more space we fill."

—LARRY SMITH, DEPUTY SECRETARY OF THE LOUISIANA DEPARTMENT OF PUBLIC SAFETY AND CORRECTIONS, 1991[1]

WITH MORE PEOPLE sent to prison in Louisiana for longer periods of time, the prison system had become overwhelmed by the end of the twentieth century. To alleviate inhumane conditions caused in part by overcrowding at Angola and the state's other prison facilities, the Loui-

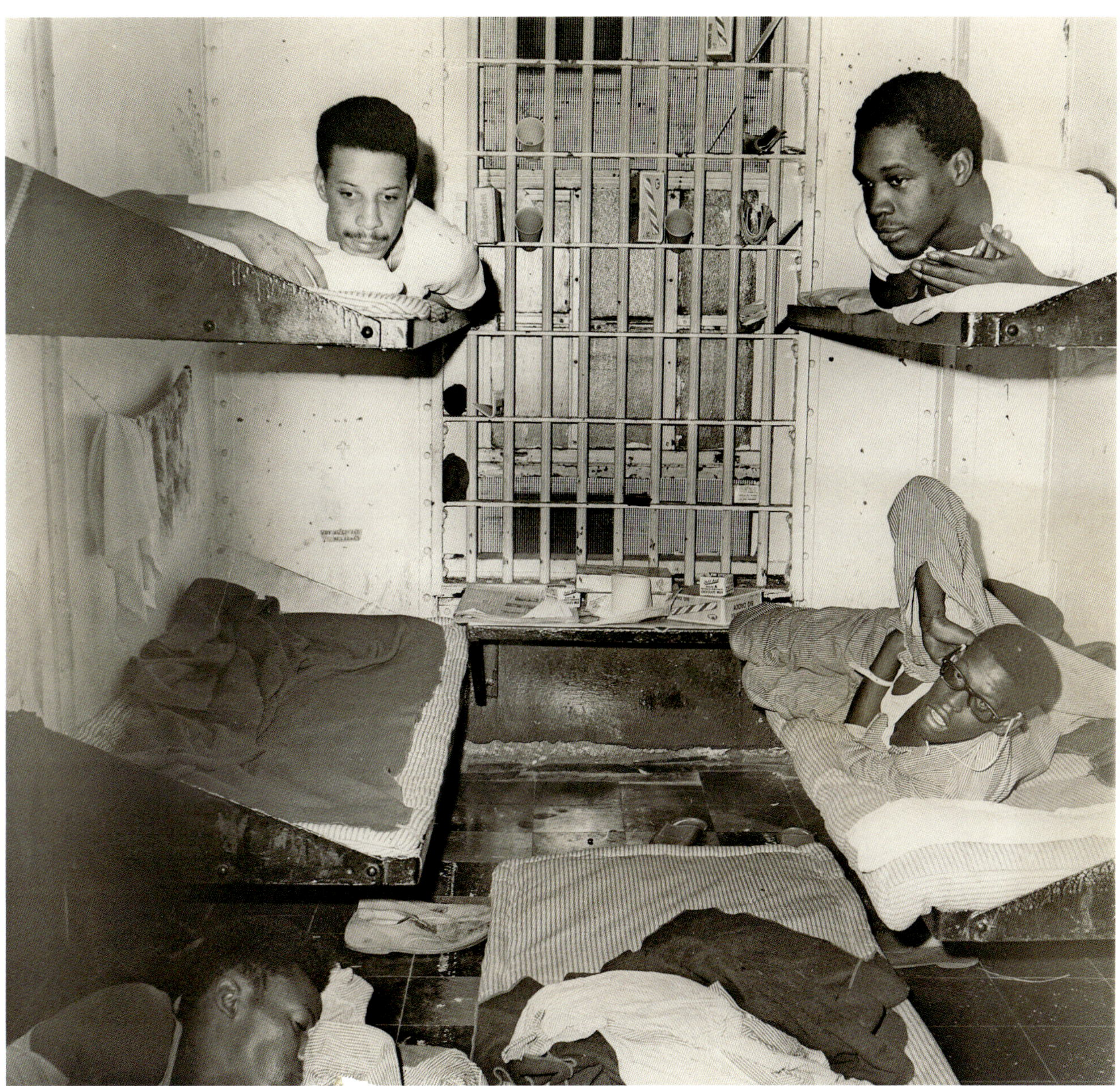

siana Department of Public Safety and Corrections began paying parish sheriff's departments to house state prisoners in local jails. This contributed to the rapid expansion of city jails—most notably the Orleans Parish jail complex at Tulane Avenue and Broad Street.

The House of Detention that had opened there in 1904 was replaced by the 450-bed Orleans Parish Prison in 1931. Capacity tripled with the addition of a new 841-bed House of Detention in 1966. Starting in the late 1970s, the parish jail complex underwent an expansion that would come

Incarcerated men at Orleans Parish Prison; May 9, 1971; gelatin silver print by Lee Delaune; *HNOC, 2020.0084.10*

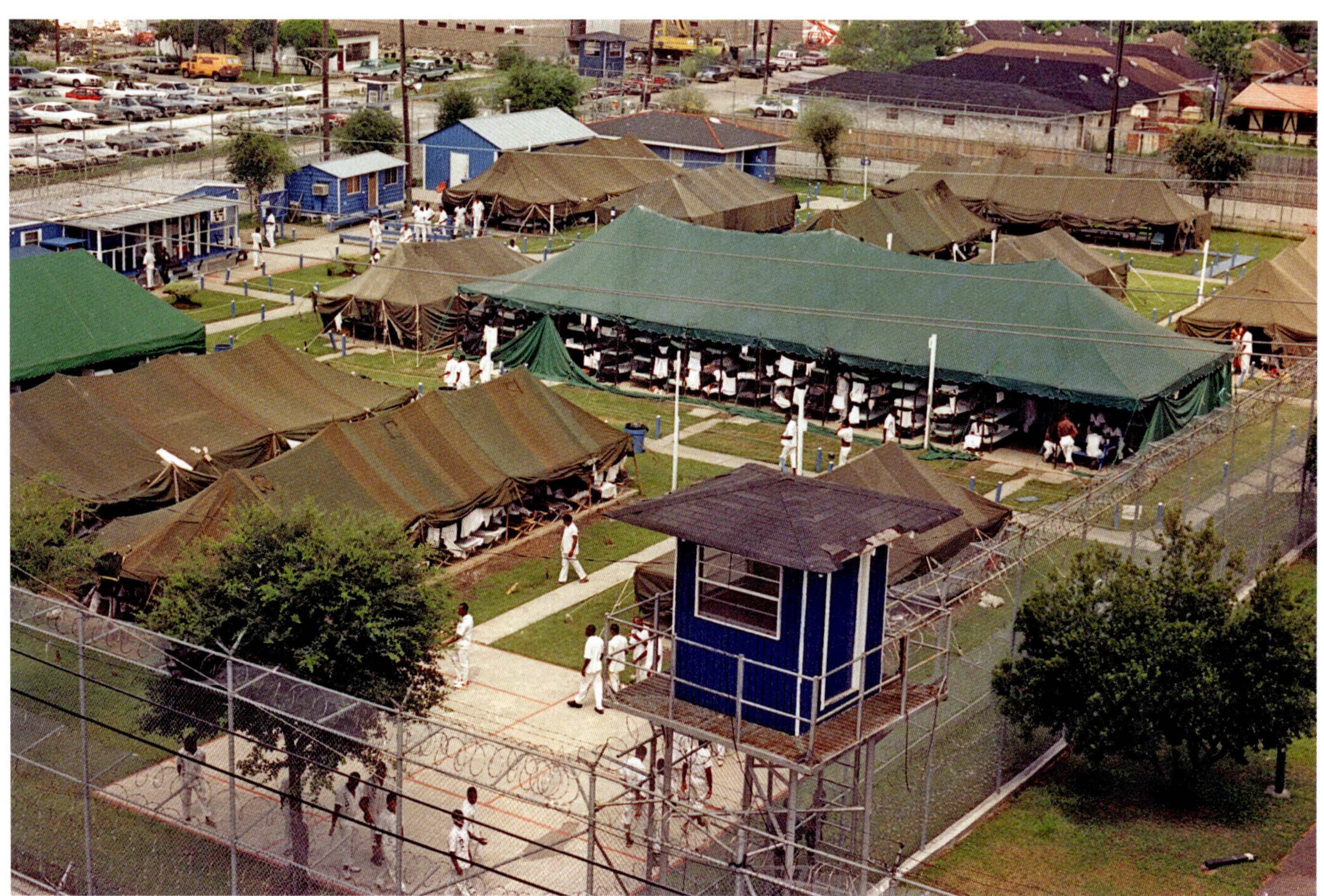

Emergency Detention Center, "Tent City," erected by Orleans Parish Sheriff Charles Foti in 1983 (detail); July 24, 1989; photograph by Ted Jackson; *HNOC, donated by NOLA Media Group, original materials © Times-Picayune, 2015.0437.62.1*

to dwarf its prior footprint. This rapid growth in jail space ran counter to a steady decline in the city's population, which peaked in the 1960s. The overcrowding crisis got so bad by 1983 that Sheriff Charles Foti put up a tented jail infamously known as "Tent City," which remained in use for nearly a decade.

In 1998, the incarcerated population at the Orleans Parish jail complex peaked at 7,495, nearly double the number of people currently held at the Louisiana State Penitentiary at Angola.

In the meantime, the city continued to construct new jail buildings. By September 1998 these facilities held 7,495 people, the most people incarcerated in New Orleans at any point and nearly double the current population of the Louisiana State Penitentiary at Angola.[2]

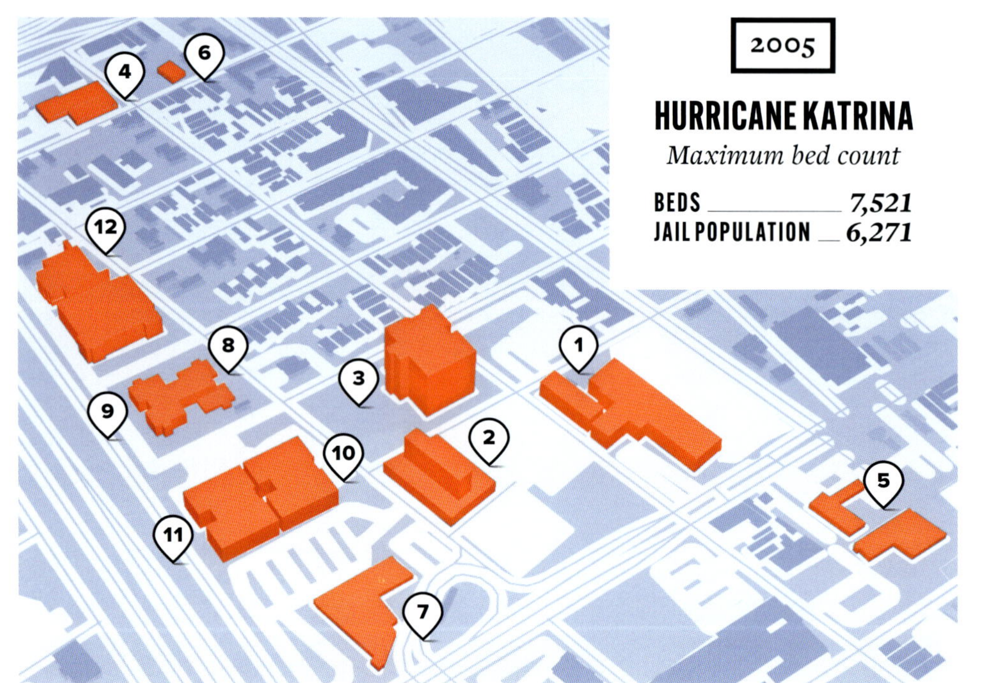

2005

HURRICANE KATRINA

Maximum bed count

BEDS *7,521*
JAIL POPULATION *6,271*

Building continued, and by Hurricane Katrina (August 2005) the area at Tulane and Broad included over a dozen separate jail facilities that housed men, women, and juveniles awaiting trial, as well as people in work-release programs and state prisoners. At its largest, in 2005, the Orleans Parish Prison campus had 7,521 beds.[3]

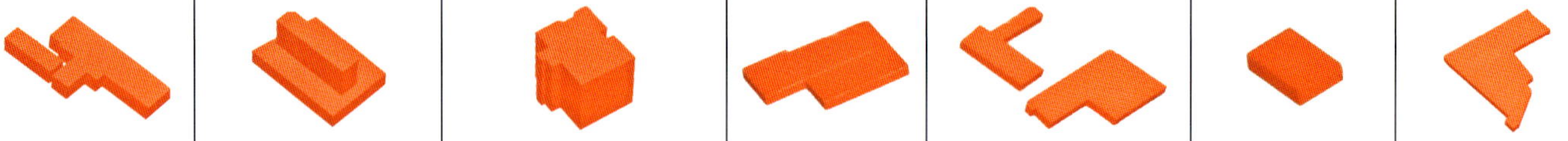

1931	1966	1977	1978	1980	1981	1991
1	2	3	4	5	6	7
ORLEANS PARISH PRISON	HOUSE OF DETENTION	COMMUNITY CORRECTIONS CENTER	FISK SCHOOL	CONCHETTA (expanded in 1992)	RENDON STREET	SOUTH WHITE STREET
450 beds	*841 beds*	*944 beds*	*150 beds*	*659 beds*	*110 beds*	*250 beds*

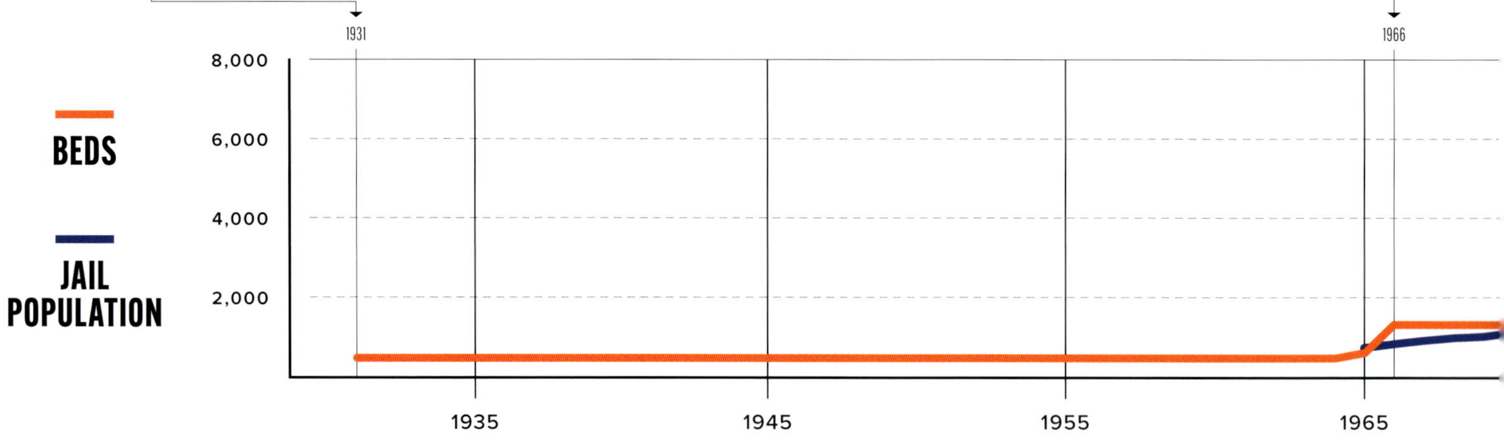

BEDS

JAIL POPULATION

1931 1966

8,000 6,000 4,000 2,000

1935 1945 1955 1965

Sheriff Marlin Gusman declined to evacuate the jail ahead of the storm, leaving the thousands of people held there to endure unimaginable horrors for days. The jail sustained major damage, accelerating a scale-down of its campus. Today the jail has a city-mandated population cap of 1,250, which it regularly exceeds.[4]

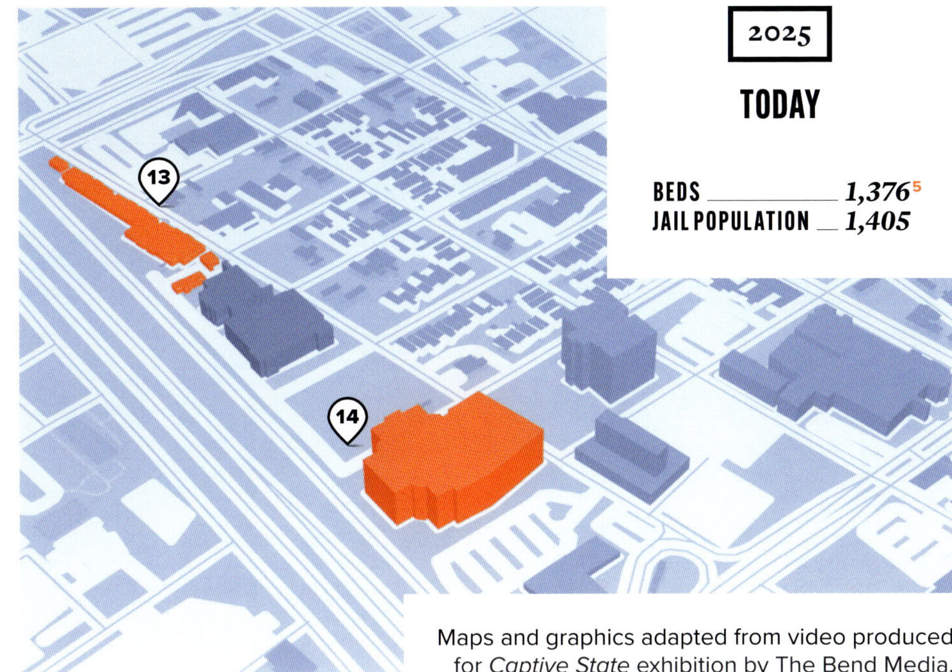

Maps and graphics adapted from video produced for *Captive State* exhibition by The Bend Media.

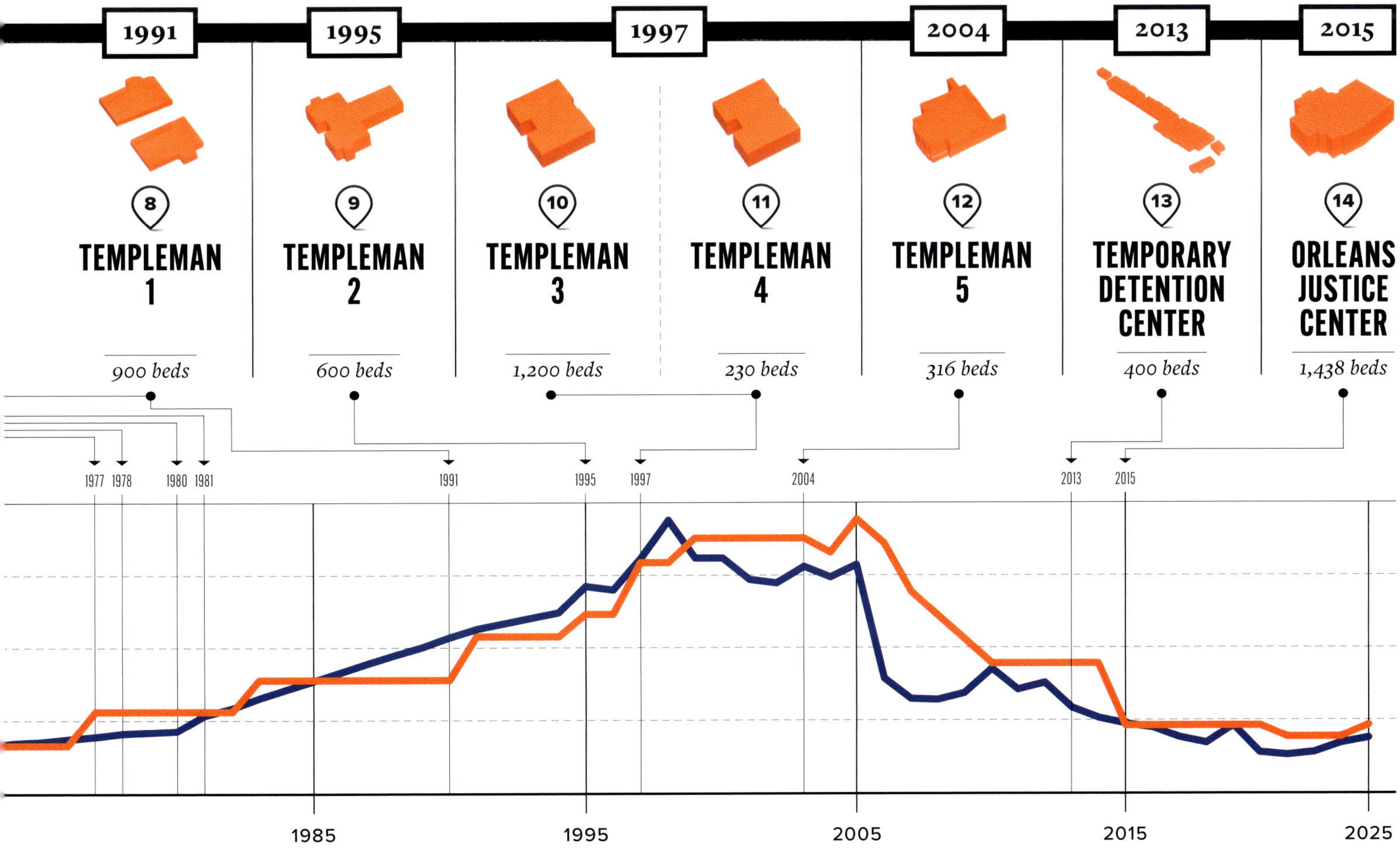

1991	1995	1997		2004	2013	2015
8	9	10	11	12	13	14
TEMPLEMAN 1	TEMPLEMAN 2	TEMPLEMAN 3	TEMPLEMAN 4	TEMPLEMAN 5	TEMPORARY DETENTION CENTER	ORLEANS JUSTICE CENTER
900 beds	*600 beds*	*1,200 beds*	*230 beds*	*316 beds*	*400 beds*	*1,438 beds*

1977 1978 1980 1981 1991 1995 1997 2004 2013 2015

1985 1995 2005 2015 2025

"They're releasing some good ones that we use every day to wash cars, to change oil in our cars, to cook in the kitchens, to do all that, where we save money."

—CADDO PARISH SHERIFF STEVE PRATOR, 2017

At its peak in 2012, the state of Louisiana incarcerated more than fifty thousand people in prisons and local jails combined. In 2017, to relieve some pressure, the state legislature passed a series of bipartisan laws signed by Gov. John Bel Edwards that allowed for the early release of hundreds of incarcerated people on good time. This rankled some officials, including then–Caddo Parish Sheriff Steve Prator, who echoed the sentiments of the New Orleans police commissioner more than a century earlier: "They're releasing some good ones that we use every day to wash cars, to change oil in our cars, to cook in the kitchens, to do all that, where we save money."[6]

Despite those efforts, more than half of the people serving sentences in Louisiana do so at local jails rather than state prisons, the highest rate in the nation.

PROFILES

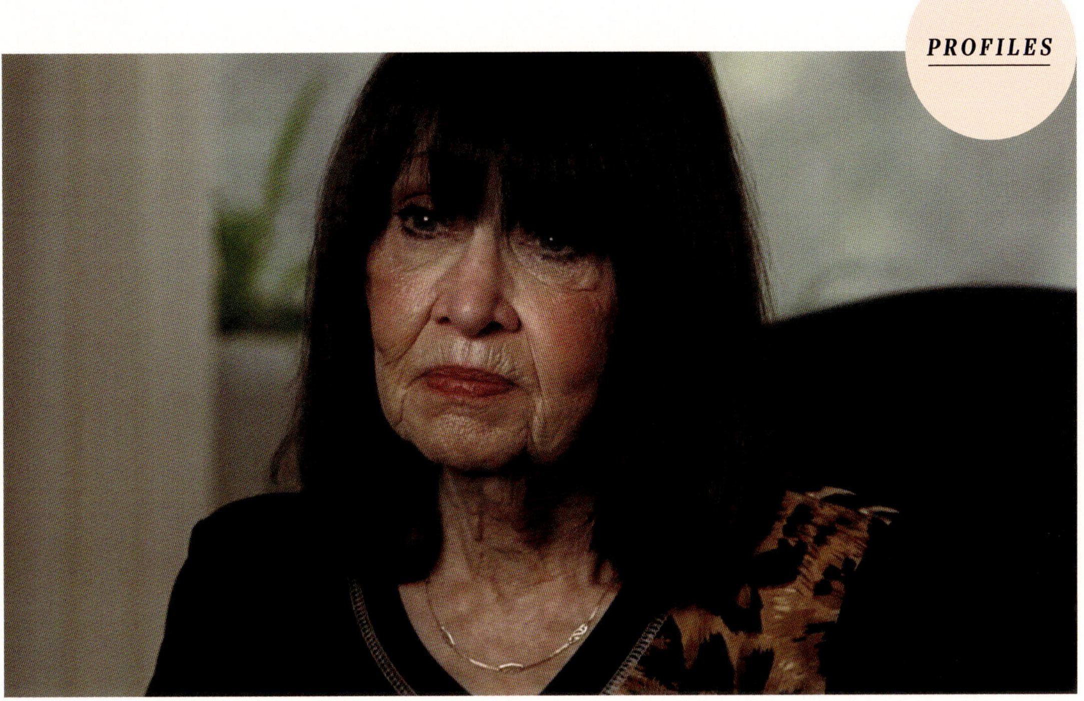

BEASY TAYLOR

"I met someone who portrayed himself as a happy-go-lucky man. He was a career batterer. There were break-ins of windows, locks, deadbolts. The night before all this began, I called police. They responded, but this time they got there before he could leave, and they made him leave. And by eleven o'clock that night, he was calling. He wanted to come get his work boots. He came to my house for his work boots, and he began attacking me. During his attack, I grabbed a knife to escape from him. I did not want him to get hurt, but he ended up dying from a stab wound. My charge was—it was second-degree murder. . . .

"They put me in housekeeping. The rule was from seven in the morning till three in the afternoon, your hand or feet or whatever part of your body would work must never stop. . . . All day long you have that side motion, where you swing the mop to the right and then back. This knee, the outer part of it, it's gone. That's all just wrecked cartilage. I later used buffing machines, floor-stripping machines—that's heavy work for my body, and I was already in my fifties."

This is excerpted from the transcript of an interview produced by the Promise of Justice Initiative, in partner ship with Decarcerate Louisiana and Professor Andrea Armstrong at Loyola University New Orleans College of Law for the End Plantation Prisons project. Taylor was released from the Louisiana Correctional Institute for Women in 2020 after serving twenty-three years in prison.

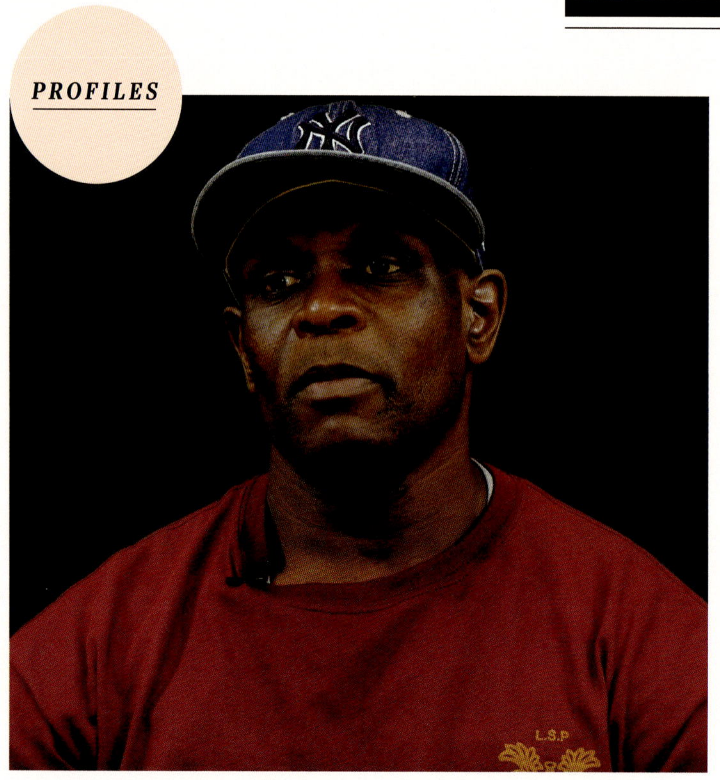

STEVEN GARNER

"Hospice is a volunteer program. But I also have a forty-hour job. I work in the library. So I have to balance those two, you know, throughout my day, plus, you know, I'm a quilter, so I sew. . . .

"When you actually give yourself to somebody and become their hands, their eyes, their feet, their mouth, their ears—when you can actually be able to give yourself to somebody, you know, you, not sending somebody for you but actually giving you to that person and his transition, I think that a great reward will be given unto that person. . . . Hospice just has been—it has been a blessing to me."

This is excerpted from the transcript of an interview conducted by the Visiting Room Project at the Louisiana State Penitentiary in 2018. Garner was released from prison four years later after serving thirty-one years. While incarcerated, he volunteered in the prison's hospice program and sewed quilts that were sold to raise money for it.

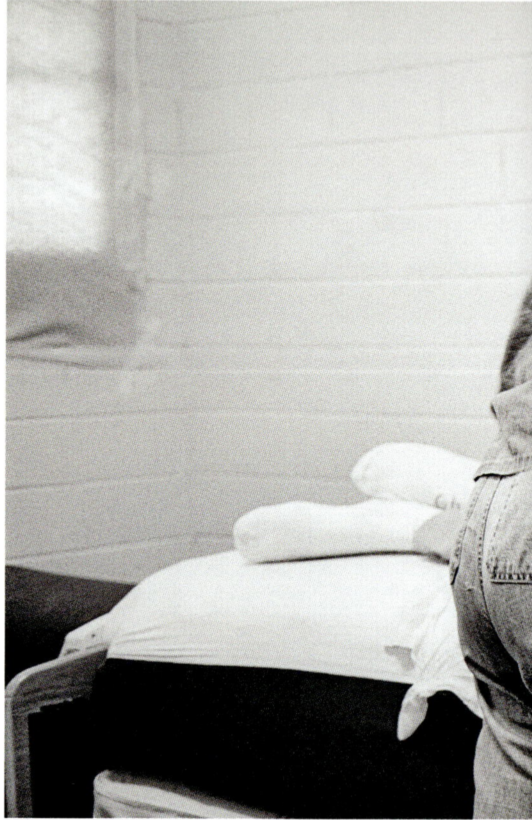

AN AGING PRISON POPULATION

THE SWELL IN PEOPLE serving life sentences without parole has resulted in an aging state prison population and more Louisianians dying while incarcerated.[7] According to the Louisiana Department of Public Safety and Corrections, 4,170 people are serving life

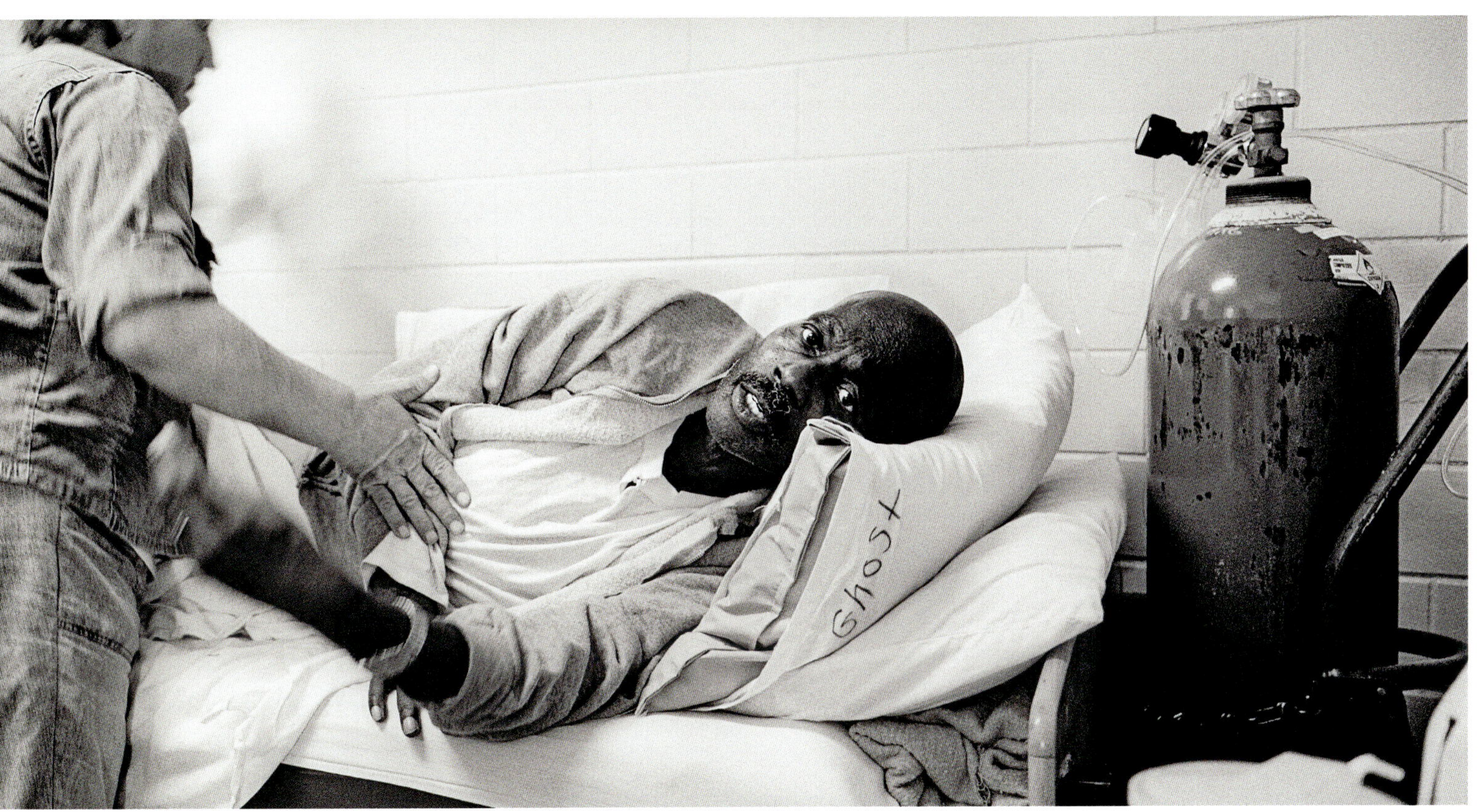

sentences in Louisiana, the vast majority of whom are Black (73 percent) and well over half of whom are fifty years or older (56 percent). At Angola, 3,392 people, or 86 percent of the population, are serving sentences exceeding fifty-one years, including those sentenced to life in prison and execution, almost all of whom will die there.[8]

In 1998 Angola began a hospice program to provide palliative care to people dying while incarcerated. The program's caregivers are incarcerated volunteers, most of whom are also sentenced to die in prison.

Calvin Helps Turn George in Bed; 2007; pigment print by Lori Waselchuk; *HNOC, 2016.0299.4*

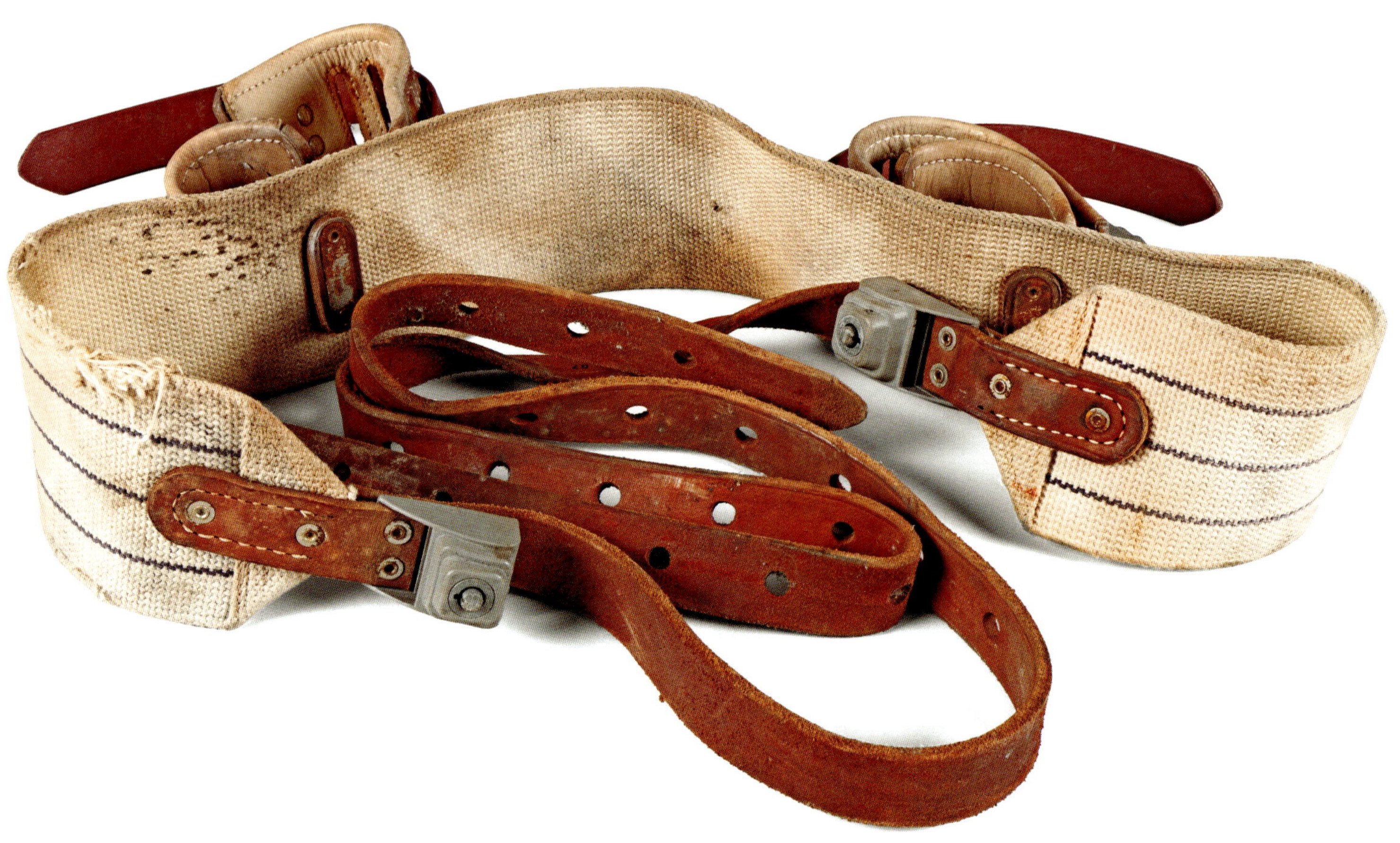

Restraints used at the House of Detention; recovered 2021; *HNOC, donated by the Orleans Parish Sheriff's Office, 2021.0183.23*

A LEGACY OF VIOLENCE

INTO THE TWENTY-FIRST CENTURY, the Orleans Parish Sheriff's Office used five-point restraints to physically immobilize people in its custody. The restraints lock people at the wrists, ankles, and waist to a "bed" made of plywood and vinyl that is bolted to the floor of an isolation cell. A restraint bed displayed in the *Captive State* exhibition was taken from the tenth floor of the House of Detention, also known as HOD-10, which served as the jail's mental health ward prior to the building's closure in 2012. HOD-10 included isolation cells and four dormitories and had no special facilities or tools for people experiencing mental health crises. They would often

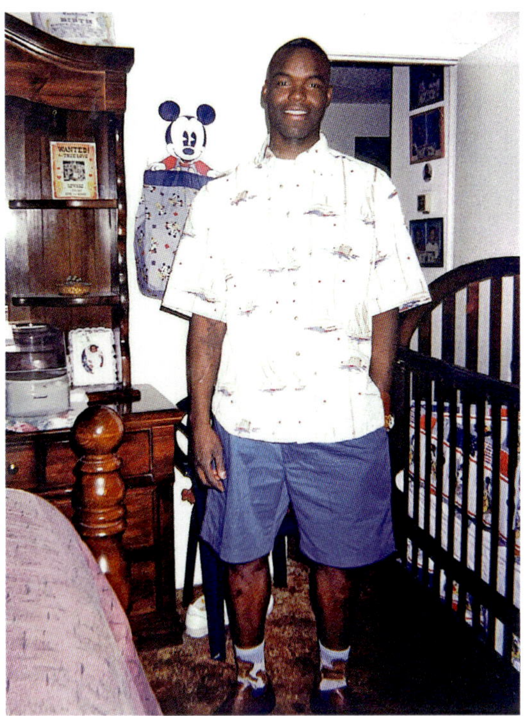

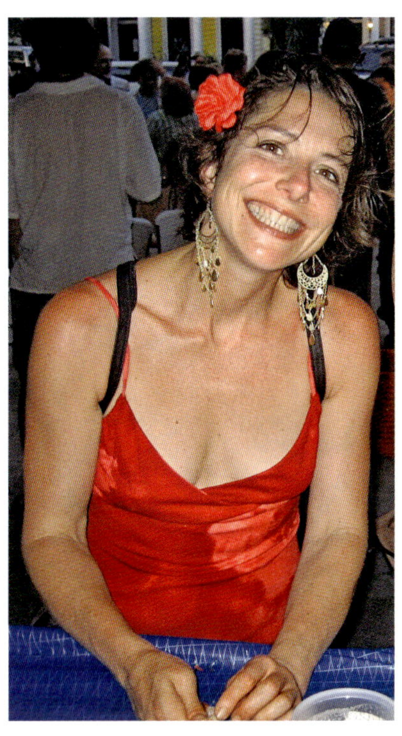

be incapacitated on restraint beds here, sometimes leading to tragic outcomes.

In 2001, twenty-four-year-old Shawn Duncan was arrested on traffic charges and sent to Orleans Parish Prison. Deemed a suicide risk, he was taken to HOD-10. Over the course of seven days, jail officials twice placed Duncan in five-point restraints. The second time, he died from dehydration after being restrained for forty-two continuous hours without adequate food, water, or medical care. In 2002 a request made by the American Civil Liberties Union to invalidate OPP's restraint policy was denied in court.[9]

In 2009 Cayne Miceli went to the hospital for an asthma attack. She was released against her will. She resisted her release, an altercation ensued, and she was arrested. At the jail, Miceli's personal items, including her inhaler, were confiscated. She continued to demand medical treatment but was denied adequate care. She was eventually sent to HOD-10 and placed in five-point restraints, where she stayed for four hours and fifteen minutes until she lost consciousness and died. An autopsy identified her cause of death as bronchial asthma.

Miceli's death was one of several highlighted by the Southern Poverty Law Center in its 2012 lawsuit against Sheriff Gusman, which led to a federal consent decree that continues to oversee the New Orleans jail. Among other things, the decree instituted strict guidelines regarding the use of restraints. Nevertheless, since 2014 at least twenty-two people have died in the jail's custody.[10]

Shawn Duncan; 2001; *courtesy of the family of Shawn Duncan*

Cayne Miceli; 2006; photograph by Misty Reilly; *courtesy of the family of Cayne Miceli*

ONE BIG SELF

"This is a document to ward off forgetting."
—Deborah Luster, 2001

Deborah Luster's photographic artwork *One Big Self: Prisoners of Louisiana* features 250 portraits of people incarcerated at three Louisiana prisons: Angola, the East Carroll Parish Prison Farm, and the Louisiana Correctional Institute for Women. Over a four-year period, Luster photographed each subject as they preferred to present themselves. Her images show people dressed in Halloween costumes, in work uniforms, with friends, and holding meaningful objects. The back of each plate includes personal details provided by the sitter. A few examples are shared here.

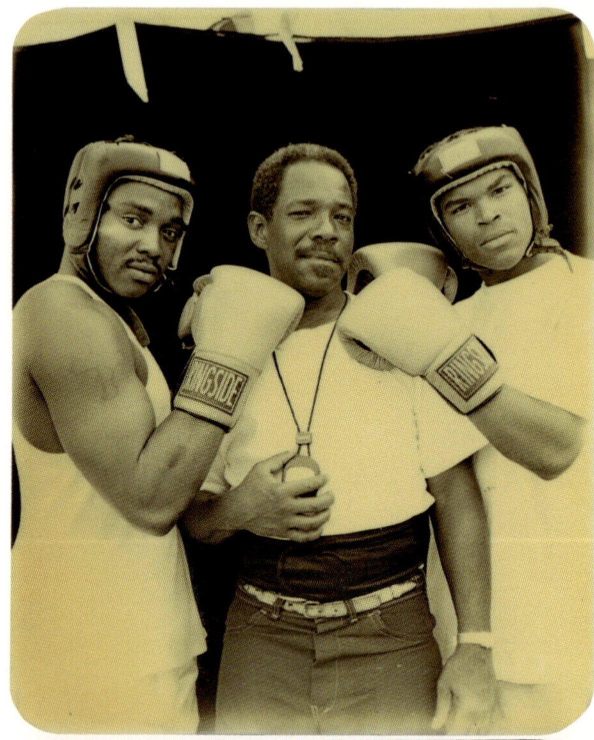

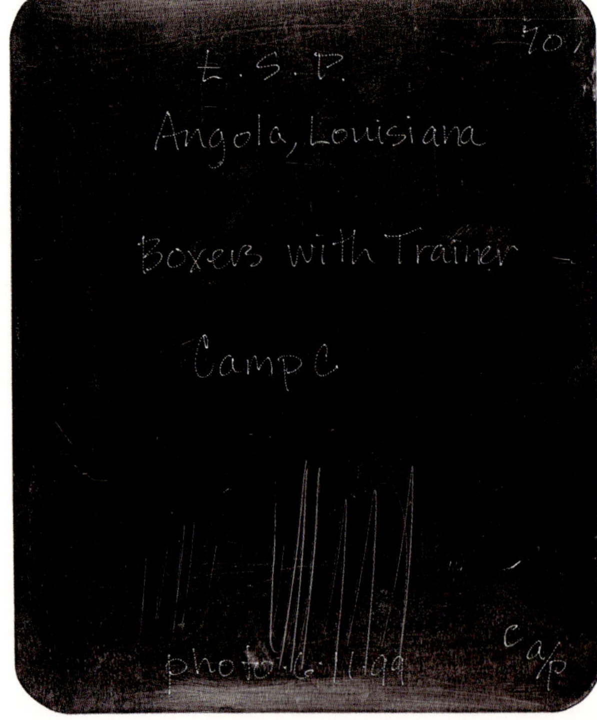

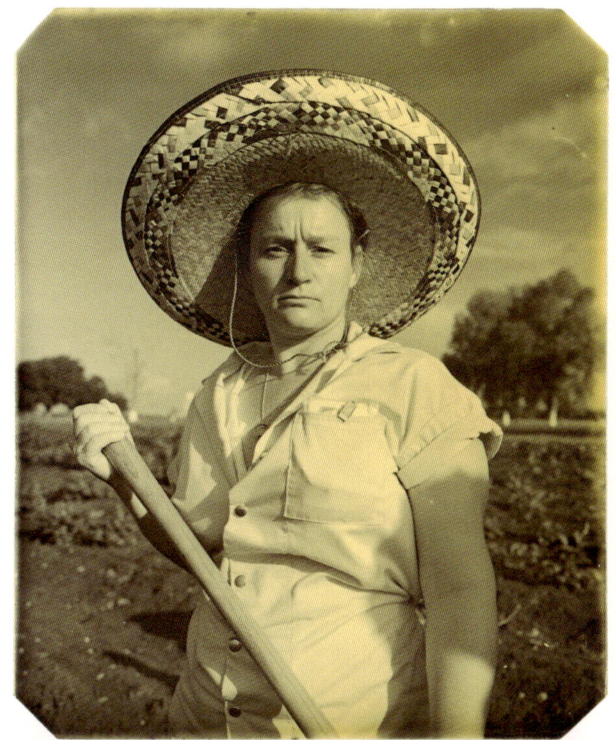

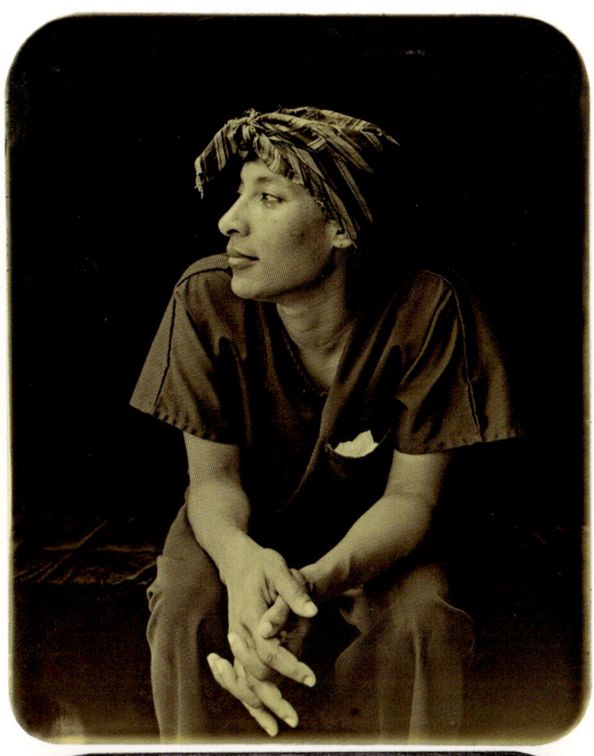

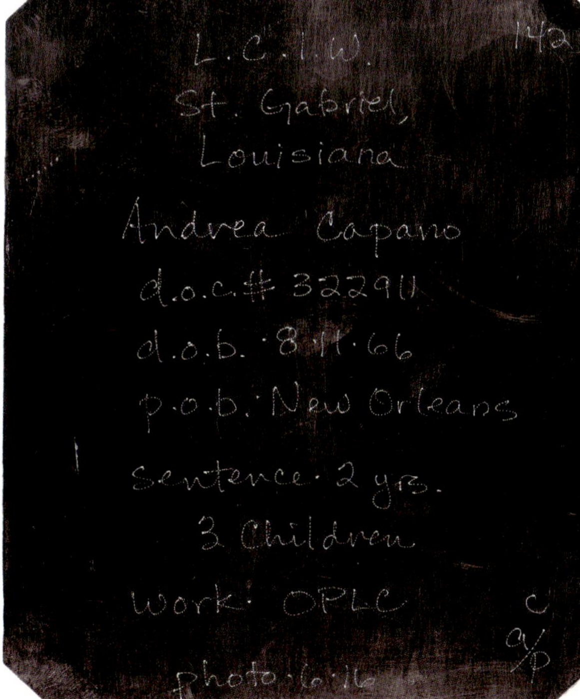

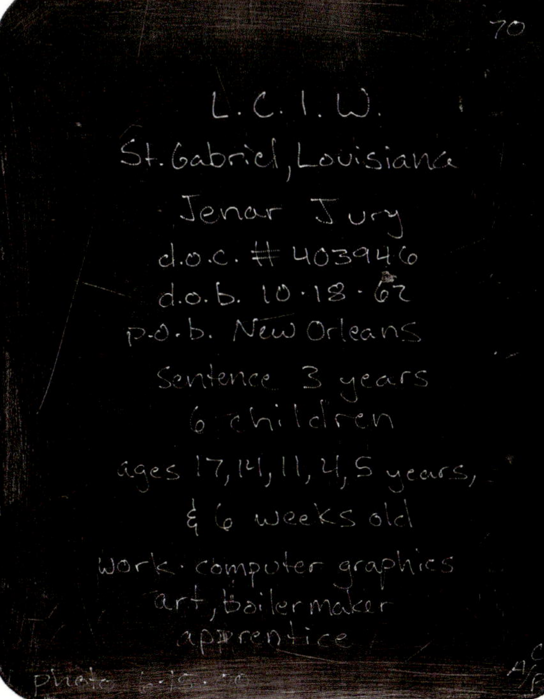

Selections from ***One Big Self: Prisoners of Louisiana***; between 1998 and 2002; silver emulsion on aluminum by Deborah Luster; *HNOC, acquisition made possible by the Laussat Society, 2023.0146.1.1–.250* (from left):

Boxers with Trainer, 1999; ***Andrea Capano***, between 1998 and 2002; ***Jenar Jury***, 2000

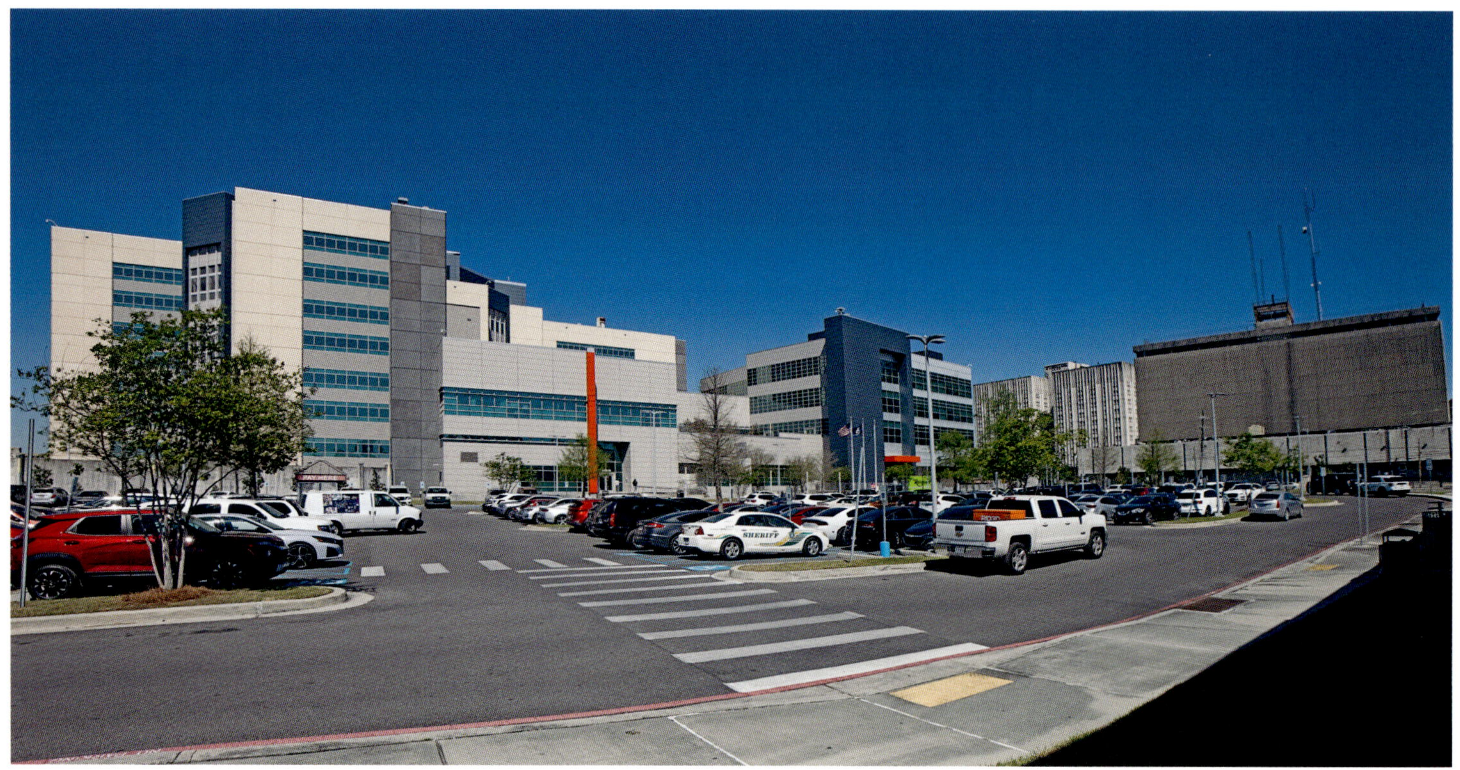

Orleans Justice Center; 2023; photograph by Keely Merritt, HNOC; *HNOC, 2023.0175.10*

ORLEANS JUSTICE CENTER

FOLLOWING HURRICANE KATRINA, a $150 million jail was built at Perdido and South Dupre Streets near Interstate 10 to replace the sprawling jail complex, much of which had been damaged in the storm and resulting flood. The new jail, commonly known as the Orleans Justice Center (OJC), has a capacity of around 1,400, a fraction of what the previous buildings could accommodate.[11]

The new jail opened without necessary operational functions, and a federal monitor's report in 2018 found it to be "critically unsafe." OJC includes no space for in-person visitation. Instead, all visitation is via teleconference, with computer terminals in a separate building across the parking lot. Despite cases like Duncan's and Miceli's, the jail also lacks federally mandated mental health facilities as of this printing. A new building with an additional eighty-nine beds is currently being built next door to fill this gap.[12]

A HUMAN AND FINANCIAL TOLL

A commitment to mass incarceration in Louisiana and New Orleans, despite declining violent crime rates, has come at a significant cost.

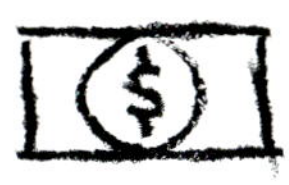

ECONOMICS

› $1.14 billion

Louisiana's total correctional costs for adults and juveniles, which includes nearly $194 million appropriated for housing adults and juveniles in the custody of the state in local jails. This does not account for the Louisiana State Police, the attorney general's office, or other criminal legal expenditures.[13]

› $24,557

The estimated annual amount paid by the state for each of the people incarcerated by the Department of Public Safety and Corrections (DOC). (Based on the DOC's reported daily "cost per offender" of $67.28 for fiscal year 2025.)[14]

› $285 million

New Orleans's 2025 budget for the New Orleans Police Department; the Orleans Parish Sheriff's Office, which operates the Orleans Justice Center; the district attorney's office; the Juvenile Justice Intervention Center; criminal and juvenile courts; and the Mayor's Office of Criminal Justice Coordination.[15]

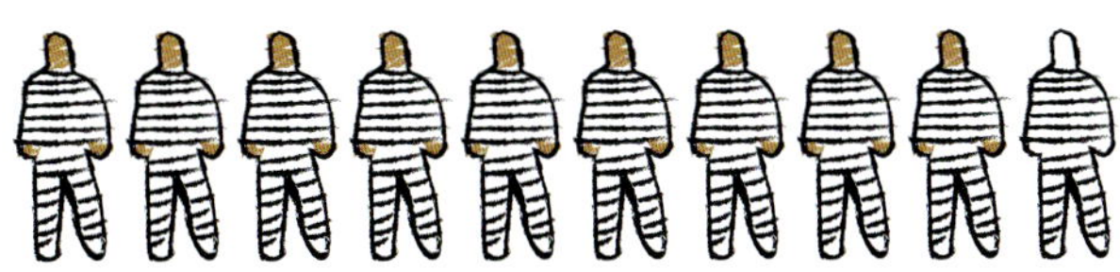

DEMOGRAPHICS[16]

The incarcerated populations in Louisiana and New Orleans are ***disproportionately Black.***

■ *Percentage of Black people in the* ***general population***

■ *Percentage of Black people in the* ***incarcerated population***

LOUISIANA

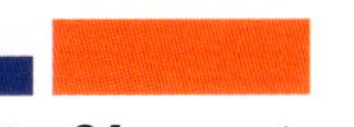

33 percent **64** percent

NEW ORLEANS

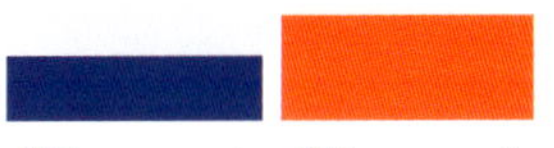

55 percent **89** percent

DEATH AND INJUSTICE[19]

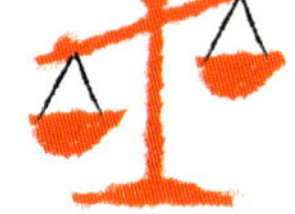

A legacy of aggressive prosecution and sentencing has resulted in an aging prison population and more people dying behind bars. Meanwhile, more people—including those serving life sentences—are exonerated from their alleged crimes in Louisiana and New Orleans than virtually anywhere else.

1,571

people **died while incarcerated** in Louisiana between 2015 and 2024.

2nd

Louisiana's national rank in **exonerations per capita** since 1989.

1st

Orleans Parish's national rank in **exonerations per capita** among counties and parishes with at least 250,000 people. Incarcerated people in New Orleans are exonerated at more than 11 times the national rate.

CRIME[17]

Violent crime is down nearly 22 percent nationwide over the last two decades, and incarceration rates have gone down 19 percent in that same time span. Violent crime is down in 37 states, and 27 of those states, including Louisiana, have reduced their incarceration rates as well. Louisiana still leads the nation in incarceration, though, in part because of the large number of people being locked up for nonviolent offenses.

▼ **14%**

Drop in Louisiana's **violent crime rate** in the last two decades.

▼ **4%**

Drop in Louisiana's **incarceration rate** in that same time.

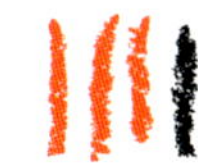

3 out of 4 ***people*** *newly incarcerated in Louisiana in 2023 were convicted or charged with a* ***nonviolent offense.***[18]

“You, now, ladies and gentlemen, have ended 138 years of Jim Crow.”

—LOUISIANA STATE SENATOR J. P. MORRELL, 2018

A NEW DAY

IN NOVEMBER 2018 Louisiana voters passed a state constitutional amendment requiring unanimous juries for conviction in criminal trials. With the approval of 64 percent of voters, the amendment overturned the state’s nonunanimous jury law that had been in place since 1880. For nearly a century and a half, the use of nonunanimous jury decisions made it much easier to convict people of felonies, while also increasing wrongful convictions that disproportionally affected people of color. By voting to amend the state constitution, Louisiana voters changed the criminal legal system and struck a blow against mass incarceration.[20] Over the centuries, Louisiana citizens have contributed to mass incarceration through their votes, their taxes, and—no less impactfully—their opinions on the meanings of race, punishment, and rehabilitation. How the system works in the future will continue to be shaped by those who call the state home.

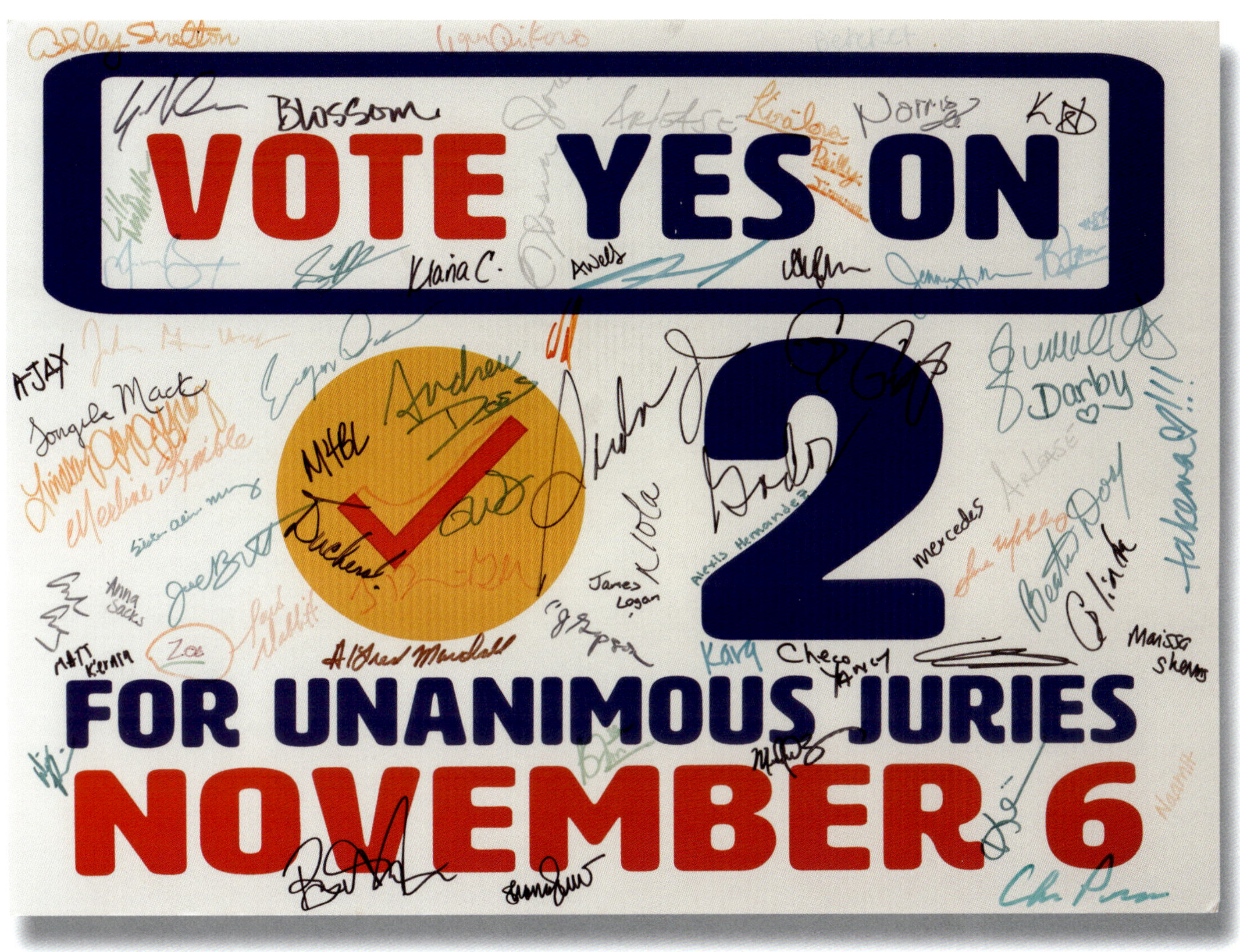

"Vote Yes on Amendment 2" yard sign, autographed by supporters; 2018; *courtesy of the Promise of Justice Initiative*

1 Michael Perlstein, "Prison-Crowding Crisis Spreads," *Times-Picayune* (New Orleans), August 4, 1991.

2 Louisiana Department of Public Safety and Corrections, Demographic Dashboard for November 30, 2024, https://doc.louisiana.gov/demographic-dashboard/. On that date, the Louisiana State Penitentiary at Angola held 3,927 people.

3 Maps and graphics adapted from "A Growing Jail District," a video produced for the *Captive State* exhibition by Jarret Lofstead and Ted Morée for The Bend Media. Data on jail expansion collected from: Orleans Parish Sheriff's Office, Campus Report, 2012, https://www.opso.us/ppt/presentation20101018.pdf; Wyma et al., *House of Detention*, 1–34; "Jail Sprawl Fences Neighborhood In," *Times-Picayune* (New Orleans), August 4, 1991; "Motel Turned Prison Will Ease Crowding," *Times-Picayune* (New Orleans), March 13, 1992; VERA Institute, "Louisiana Locked Up: A Problem in Every Parish," https://www.vera.org/louisiana-locked-up; New Orleans City Council, Jail Population Dashboard, https://council.nola.gov/dashboards/; "Special Committee Reports Findings on Parish Prison," *Louisiana Weekly*, February 27, 1965; "Inmate Transfer Begins," *Times-Picayune/States-Item* (New Orleans), October 3, 1981; and "Foti Seeks Bond Issue for Jail Space," *Times-Picayune* (New Orleans), September 1, 1999.

4 National Prison Project, *Abandoned and Abused*, 29–59.

5 La'Shance Perry, "'It Isn't Very Clear Who is Responsible for the Jail Getting to That Cap,'" *The Lens* (New Orleans), June 21, 2024. Though the Orleans Justice Center opened with a stated capacity of 1,438 beds, it has since been reduced to 1,376. The Temporary Detention Center opened with a capacity of 400 but as of June 13, 2024, housed only 75 incarcerated people.

6 Jonah E. Bromwich, "Louisiana Sheriff's Remarks Evoke Slavery, Critics Say," *New York Times*, October 12, 2017.

7 Turner, *A Living Death*, 23; Nellis, *Still Life*, 10, 15.

8 Louisiana Department of Public Safety and Corrections, Demographic Dashboard for November 30, 2024, https://doc.louisiana.gov/demographic-dashboard/.

9 American Civil Liberties Union, "ACLU Raises Concerns over Psychiatric Services after Suicide at Orleans Parish Prison," press release, June 8, 2004.

10 Mary Howell, "40 and Counting . . . : Orleans Parish Prison Deaths Since 2006," presentation given to the New Orleans City Council, August 2012; United States District Court Eastern District of Louisiana, Consent Judgment in *Lashawn Jones, et al., and the United States of America v. Marlin Gusman*, Civil Action No. 12-00859 Section 1, 2013.

11 Kelsey Davis, "Orleans Parish Sheriff's Office Completes Inmate Transfer to New Facility," WDSU News, September 15, 2015.

12 Matt Sledge, "Brutal Federal Monitors' Report Says New Orleans Jail Is 'Critically Unsafe' Despite Slight Improvement," *The Advocate* (New Orleans), January 18, 2018; Nick Chrastil, "How Phase III Came to Be," *The Lens* (New Orleans), January 2, 2024.

13 Governor Jeff Landry and Commissioner of Administration Taylor Barras, "State of Louisiana State Budget: Fiscal Year 2024–2025," 125, 149, 243–45. Total appropriations for these categories for fiscal year 2024–25 are $1,141,248,939.

14 Louisiana Department of Public Safety and Corrections, "Budget and Cost Data Summary FY 2025 Act 4 (Excluding Canteen and Rodeo)," July 1, 2024, https://doc.louisiana.gov/wp-content/uploads/2024/11/od-Budget-Human-Resources-PE-Website.pdf.

15 City of New Orleans, "2025 Adopted Annual Operating Budget," accessed February 12, 2025, https://nola.openbook.questica.com.

16 New Orleans City Council, Jail Population Dashboard for December 18, 2024, https://council.nola.gov/dashboards/; Louisiana Department of Public Safety and Corrections, Demographic Dashboard for November 30, 2024, https://doc.louisiana.gov/demographic-dashboard/; US Census Bureau, Louisiana state profile, data.census.gov.

17 Federal Bureau of Investigation Crime Data Explorer, Summary Reporting System, "Estimated Crimes 1979–2023," cde.ucr.cjis.gov; Prison Policy Initiative, "Appendix Table 5, Jail and Prison Incarceration Populations by State, 1978–2022," 2024, https://www.prisonpolicy.org/reports/jails2024_table5.html. Violent crime and incarceration rates were calculated per 100,000 residents; violent crime rates in 2023 were compared to 2003, and incarceration rates in 2022 were compared to 2003, due to incomplete incarceration data for 2023. For more on the relationship between incarceration and crime, see Stemen, *The Prison Paradox*.

18 Louisiana Department of Public Safety and Corrections, "Incarceration Reason by Crime Type" in Admissions Dashboard for 2023, https://doc.louisiana.gov/admissions-dashboard/. Of the 14,399 people admitted to the Louisiana Department of Corrections in 2023, 10,731 (75 percent) were admitted for nonviolent offenses.

19 Loyola University New Orleans College of Law, Incarceration Transparency,"Louisiana Deaths Behind Bars: All Parish Data," https://www.incarcerationtransparency.org/la-prison-and-jail-deaths-all-parish-data/. Exoneration data as of November 19, 2024, courtesy of the National Registry of Exonerations, a project of the Newkirk Center for Science and Society at University of California Irvine, the University of Michigan Law School, and Michigan State University College of Law. Per-capita rates calculated using US Census Bureau population data for 2023.

20 Julia O'Donoghue, "Louisiana Approves Unanimous Jury Requirement, Scrapping Jim Crow–Era Law," *Times-Picayune* (New Orleans), November 7, 2018; Southern Center for Human Rights, "The End of Louisiana's 'Jim Crow Jury,'" press release, November 16, 2018.

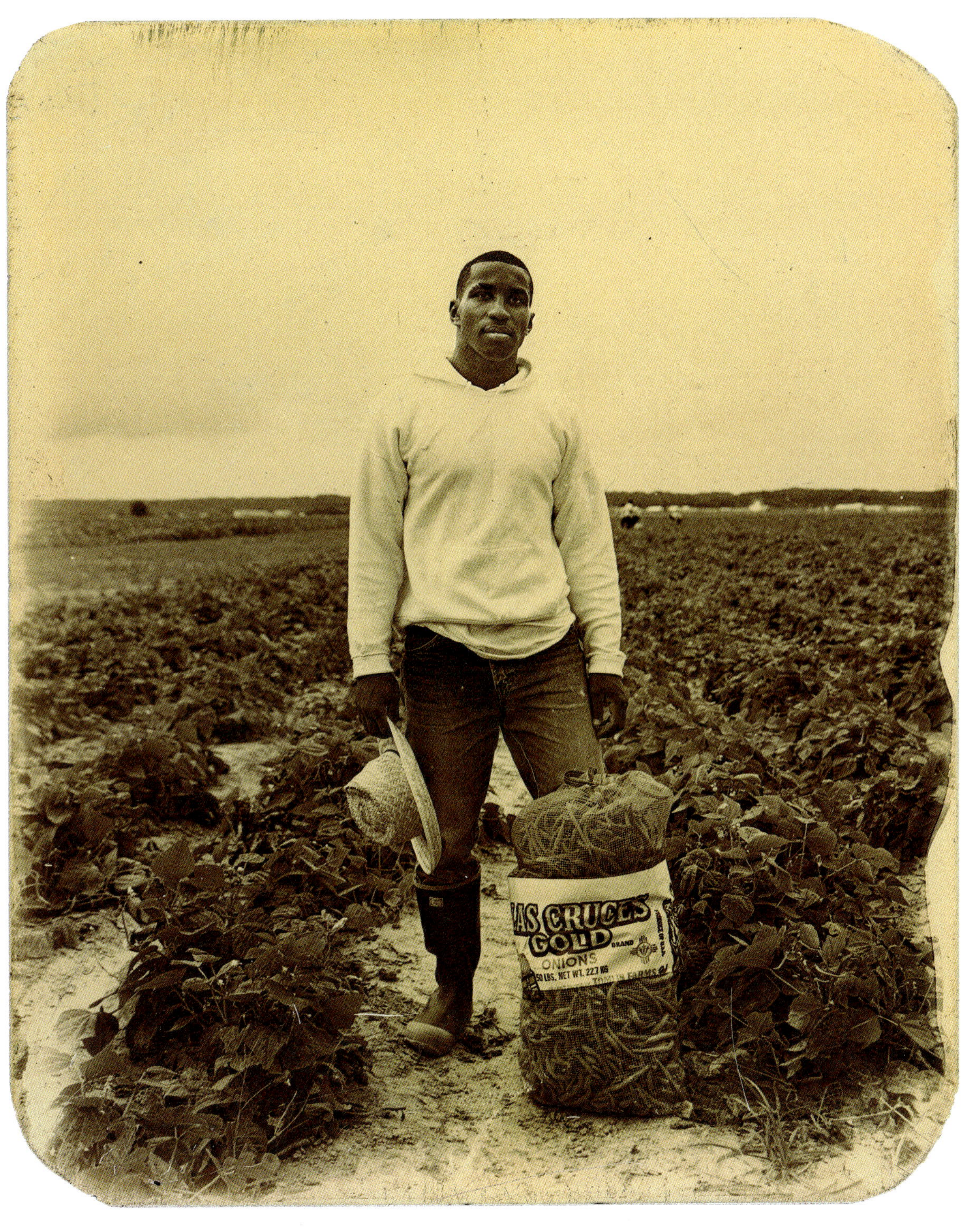

Troy West from ***One Big Self: Prisoners of Louisiana***; 1999; silver emulsion on aluminum; by Deborah Luster; *HNOC, acquisition made possible by the Laussat Society, 2023.0146.1.168*

Epilogue

REFLECTION AND ACTION

"Begin with empathy."

—A VISITOR TO THE *CAPTIVE STATE* EXHIBITION

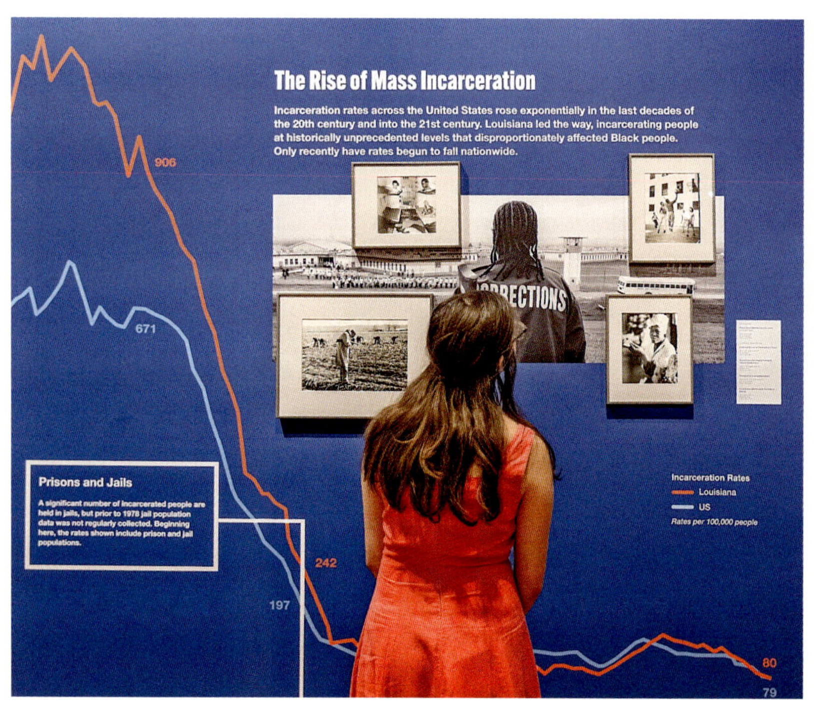

THROUGHOUT THE RUN of the *Captive State* exhibition, visitors weighed in on this question: If you could change Louisiana's incarceration system, where would you begin? Thousands of people shared their opinions, and selected responses are displayed on the following pages.

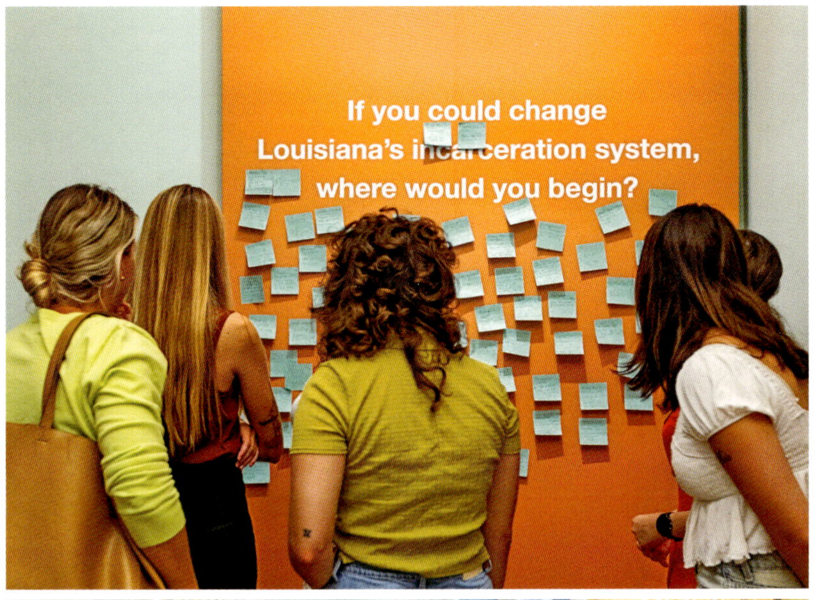

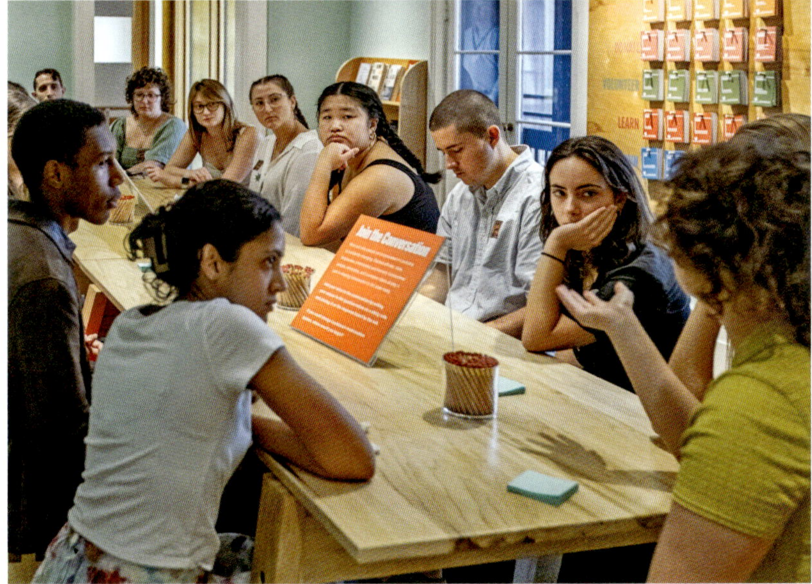

Visitors and tour groups to *Captive State* weighed in on a reflection question and held discussions after viewing the exhibition. Photographs by Amber Johnson, HNOC.

For those looking for ways they can spark change and learn more about issues related to mass incarceration, the Historic New Orleans Collection has curated a list of local and national resources that can be viewed at https://hnoc.org/captive-state-resources.

The bibliography that begins on page 98 lists the publications referenced during the curation of the exhibition and production of this book, and is an excellent place to start for those looking to research mass incarceration in more depth.

GET RID OF THE DEATH SENTENCE

-More educational programs.

-A LIVABLE WAGE.

In the Library

end mandatory minimums

FUND EDUCATION

The safest cities have the MOST resources, not the most police & prisons. Invest in your communities!!

Enseñando a los niños sobre la tolerancia y la riqueza de la diversidad

Start talking to everyone about it. That seems like a beginning that doesn't feel overwhelming.

ABOLITION End plantation slavery - nuff said.

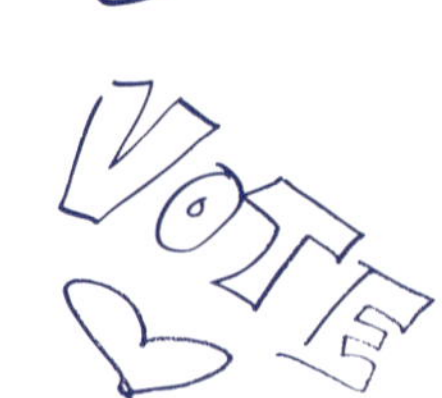

If you could change Louisiana's incarceration system,

End Solitary Confinement

ADOPT A RESTORATIVE JUSTICE PROGRAM!

SCHOOL TO PRISON PIPELINE

COMPASSION

Giving inmates (including felons) the right to vote.

- Increase mental health facilities
- focus on education
- end generational poverty
- close loopholes

Mercy

Provide fair & equal access to FOOD & HEALTH CARE. Change starts caring!

HUMANITY

Mutual Aid Now!

RESPECT.

MORE INPUT & HELP FOR YOUNG PEOPLE WITH MENTAL HEALTH AND CPTSD FROM TRAUMATIZED CHILDHOODS

end the "war on drugs"

Cambiar la mentalidad racista y de supremacia blanca.

Enfoque descolonial

LOVE

freeing all incarcerated individuals who were convicted by nonunanimous juries.

todos los ciudadanos deben ser tratados por igual. No importa su COLOR.

Acaso estamos enfermos mentalmente?

END for profit and private incarceration facilities

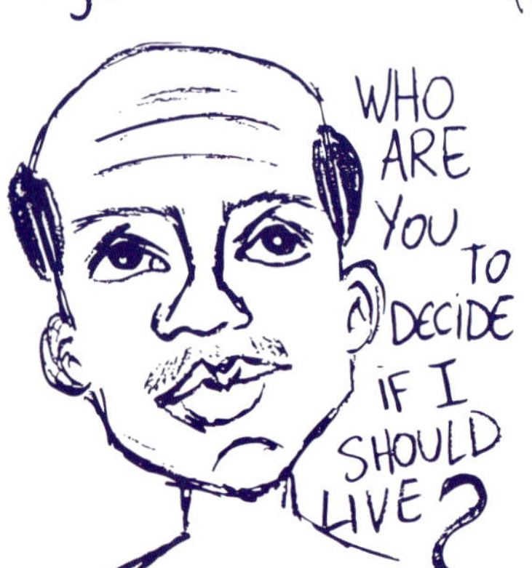

Vote Vote Vote RUN!!

LEGALIZE MARIHUANA

& RELEASE ALL THOSE CONVICTED FOR POSSESSION etc.!

where would you begin?

Let the aging prisoners out!

ADEQUATE OF FUNDING PUBLIC DEFENSE

Abolition now

End Poverty

Listen + talk to formerly incarcerated people. Learn from those closest & most impacted by the carceral state.

Make people understand the radical notion that all people are people.

Fund public health & housing for all ♡

Kindergarten

CLASS CONSCIENCE ♥

I am a public school teacher. Support families and children at early ages. And when families show signs of struggle.

Term limits for DA's & Sheriffs

Ne pas oublier que ce sont des personnes qu'on incarcère. Toutes ont un droit à la dignité et à la protection.

CHANGE THE 13TH AMENDMENT

PAY REPARATIONS

Education!!!

Using my voice to tell others!

BAN PRIVATIZED PRISONS!

Root out White supremacy

Liberté Humanité Respect ♡

Admit There is a problem

Free Them All

INVEST IN SOCIAL SERVICES, Education - FREE PREK! KEEP KIDS OUT OF JAIL

Social Emotional Learning

Re-allocate Prison funds to education funds

myself.

zero tolerance for complacency.

END SLAVERY TODAY!

REHABILITATION NOT INCARCERATION

Therapy

Make Just trials available to ALL. NOT JUST the Rich.

Begin with empathy.

Take steps to dismantle systemic racism that feeds the prison industrial complex

MORE ACCOUNTABILITY FOR PROSECUTORS

May Almight God help us to be thy Brother's Keeper!

focus on humanity and justice, not punishment and confinement

END CASH BAIL

TRAIN TEACHERS

AFTER SCHOOL PROGRAMS

Stop incarceration for non-violent offenses

Bibliography

Acts and Deliberations of the Cabildo, 1769–1803. Microfilm of English translations by the Works Progress Administration. New Orleans City Archives and Special Collections, New Orleans Public Library.

Aiello, Thomas. *Jim Crow's Last Stand: Nonunanimous Criminal Jury Verdicts in Louisiana*. Louisiana State University Press, 2015.

Alexander, Michelle. *The New Jim Crow: Mass Incarceration in the Age of Colorblindness.* New Press, 2010.

Armstrong, Andrea. *The Impact of 300 Years of Jail Conditions.* The Data Center, 2018.

Aslakson, Kenneth R. *Making Race in the Courtroom: The Legal Construction of Three Races in Early New Orleans.* New York University Press, 2014.

Ayers, Edward L. *Vengeance and Justice: Crime and Punishment in the Nineteenth-Century American South*. Oxford University Press, 1984.

Bardes, John. *The Carceral City: Slavery and the Making of Mass Incarceration in New Orleans, 1803–1930.* University of North Carolina Press, 2024.

Bardes, John. "Mass Incarceration in the Age of Slavery and Emancipation: Fugitive Slaves, Poor Whites, and Prison Development in Louisiana, 1805–1877." PhD diss., Tulane University, 2020.

Bardes, John. "Sailing While Black." *64 Parishes*, Spring 2020.

Beck, Allen J. *Bureau of Justice Statistics Bulletin: Prisoners in 1999*. US Department of Justice, 2000.

Birch, Kelly. "Slavery and the Origins of Louisiana's Prison Industry, 1803–1861." PhD diss., University of Adelaide, 2017.

Birch, Kelly, and Thomas C. Buchanan. "The Penalty of a Tyrant's Law: Landscapes of Incarceration During the Second Slavery." *Slavery and Abolition* 34, no. 1 (2013): 22–38.

Blackmon, Douglas A. *Slavery by Another Name:*

The Re-Enslavement of Black Americans from the Civil War to World War II. Doubleday, 2008.

Bowie, Chet. *Bureau of Justice Statistics Bulletin: Prisoners 1925–81*. US Department of Justice, 1982.

Carleton, Mark T. *Politics and Punishment: The History of the Louisiana State Penal System*. Louisiana State University Press, 1984.

Carleton, Mark T. "The Politics of the Convict Lease System in Louisiana: 1868–1901." *Louisiana History* 8, no. 1 (1967): 5–25.

Carson, E. Ann. *Bureau of Justice Statistics Bulletin: Prisoners in 2016*. US Department of Justice, 2018.

Carson, E. Ann. *Bureau of Justice Statistics Bulletin: Prisoners in 2019*. US Department of Justice, 2020.

Carson, E. Ann. *Bureau of Justice Statistics Statistical Tables: Prisoners in 2021*. US Department of Justice, 2022.

Carson, E. Ann, and Rich Kluckow. *Bureau of Justice Statistics Statistical Tables: Prisoners in 2022*. US Department of Justice, 2023.

Carson, E. Ann, and William J. Sabol. *Bureau of Justice Statistics Bulletin: Prisoners in 2011*. US Department of Justice, 2012.

Carter, Clarence Edwin, ed. *The Territorial Papers of the United States*. Vol. 9. United States Government Printing Office, 1940.

Clifton, Ellis, and Rebecca Ginsburg, eds. *Slavery in the City: Architecture and Landscapes of Urban Slavery in North America*. University of Virginia Press, 2017.

Courtwright, David T. *Violent Land: Single Men and Social Disorder from the Frontier to the Inner City*. Harvard University Press, 1996.

Dawdy, Shannon Lee. "The Burden of Louis Congo and the Evolution of Savagery in Colonial Louisiana." In *Discipline and the Other Body: Correction, Corporeality, Colonialism*, edited by Steven Pierce and Anupama Rao, 61–89. Duke University Press, 2006.

De Beaumont, Gustave, and Alexis de Tocqueville. *On the Penitentiary System in the United States and Its Application in France*. Translated by Francis Lieber. Philadelphia, 1833.

De Koster, Margo, and Herbert Reinke. "Policing Minorities." In *The Oxford Handbook of the History of Crime and Criminal Justice*, edited by Paul Knepper and Anja Johansen, 268–84. Oxford University Press, 2016.

Derbes, Brett Josef. "'Secret Horrors': Enslaved Women and Children in the Louisiana State Penitentiary, 1833–1862." *The Journal of African American History* 98, no. 2 (2013): 277–90.

Din, Gilbert C., and John E. Harkins. *The New Orleans Cabildo: Colonial Louisiana's First City Government, 1769–1803*. Louisiana State University Press, 1996.

Forret, Jeff. "Before Angola: Enslaved Prisoners in the Louisiana State Penitentiary." *Louisiana History* 54, no. 2 (2013): 133–71.

Gilliard, Darrell K., and Allen J. Beck. *Bureau of Justice Statistics Bulletin: Prisoners in 1997*. US Department of Justice, 1998.

Goluboff, Risa. *Vagrant Nation: Police Power, Constitutional Change, and the Making of the 1960s*. Oxford University Press, 2016.

Greenfeld, Lawrence A. *Bureau of Justice Statistics Bulletin: Prisoners in 1989*. US Department of Justice, 1990.

Hair, William Ivy. "Bourbon Democracy." In *Louisiana Politics and the Paradoxes of Reaction and Reform, 1877–1928*, Louisiana Purchase Bicentennial Series in Louisiana History 7, edited by Matthew J. Schott, 115–41. University of Louisiana Press, 2000.

Hall, Aaron R. "Public Slaves and State Engineers: Modern Statecraft on Louisiana's Waterways, 1833–1861." *Journal of Southern History* 85, no. 3 (2019): 531–76.

Hallinan, Joseph T. *Going Up the River: Travels in a Prison Nation.* Random House, 2001.

Harrison, Paige M., and Allen J. Beck. *Bureau of Justice Statistics Bulletin: Prisoners in 2003.* US Department of Justice, 2004.

Hirsch, Adam Jay. *The Rise of the Penitentiary: Prisons and Punishment in Early America.* Yale University Press, 1992.

Huber, Leonard V., and Samuel Wilson Jr. *The Cabildo on Jackson Square.* Pelican, 1970.

Incarceration Transparency Project. *Louisiana Deaths Behind Bars: 2015–2021.* Loyola University New Orleans College of Law, 2023.

Ingersoll, Thomas N. *Mammon and Manon in Early New Orleans: The First Slave Society in the Deep South, 1718–1819.* University of Tennessee Press, 1999.

Johnson, Rashauna. *Slavery's Metropolis: Unfree Labor in New Orleans during the Age of Revolutions.* Cambridge University Press, 2016.

Langan, Patrick A., John V. Fundis, Lawrence A. Greenfeld, and Victoria W. Schneider. *Historical Statistics on Prisoners in State and Federal Institutions, Yearend 1925–1986.* US Department of Justice, 1988.

Le Glaunec, Jean-Pierre. "Slave Migrations and Slave Control in New Orleans." In *Empires of the Imagination: Transatlantic Histories of the Louisiana Purchase,* edited by Peter J. Kastor and François Weil, 204–38. University of Virginia Press, 2009.

LeFlouria, Talitha L. *Chained in Silence: Black Women and Convict Labor in the New South.* University of North Carolina Press, 2015.

Louisiana. *Official Journal of the Proceedings of the Constitutional Convention of the State of Louisiana: Held in New Orleans, Tuesday, February 8, 1898.* New Orleans, 1898. HathiTrust.

Louisiana. *Report of the Senate Committee on Penitentiary, to the Senate, Session 1878.* New Orleans, 1878. Google Books.

Louisiana Department of Public Safety and Corrections. *Briefing Book: July 2023 Update.* Louisiana Department of Public Safety and Corrections, 2023.

Mancini, Matthew J. *One Dies, Get Another: Convict Leasing in the American South, 1866–1928.* University of South Carolina Press, 1996.

Manion, Jen. *Liberty's Prisoners: Carceral Culture in Early America.* University of Pennsylvania Press, 2015.

Masur, Louis P. *Rites of Execution: Capital Punishment and the Transformation of American Culture, 1776–1865.* Oxford University Press, 1989.

McGoldrick, Stacy K. "The Policing of Slavery in New Orleans, 1852–1860." *Journal of Historical Sociology* 14, no. 4 (2001): 397–417.

Mueller, Derek. *Bureau of Justice Statistics Prisons Report Series: Preliminary Data Release, 2023.* US Department of Justice, 2024.

National Criminal Justice Information and Statistics Service. *The Nation's Jails: A Report on the Census of Jails from the 1972 Survey of Inmates of Local Jails.* US Department of Justice, 1975.

National Criminal Justice Information and Statistics Service. *National Jail Census, 1970.* US Department of Justice, 1971.

National Prison Project. *Abandoned and Abused: Orleans Parish Prisoners in the Wake of Hurricane Katrina.* American Civil Liberties Union, 2006.

Nellis, Ashley. *Still Life: America's Increasing Use of Life and Long-Term Sentences.* The Sentencing Project, 2017.

Novak, Daniel. *The Wheel of Servitude: Black Forced Labor after Slavery.* University Press of Kentucky, 1978.

Oshinsky, David M. *"Worse Than Slavery": Parchman Farm and the Ordeal of Jim Crow Justice.* Free Press, 1996.

Reichel, Philip L. "Southern Slave Patrols

as a Transitional Police Type." *American Journal of Police* 7, no. 2 (1988): 51–78.

Roberts, Ginger. "Edward Livingston and American Penology." *Louisiana Law Review* 37, no. 5 (1977): 1037–67.

Rousey, Dennis Charles. *Policing the Southern City: New Orleans, 1805–1889*. Louisiana State University Press, 1996.

Ryan, Joanne, and Stephanie L. Perrault. *Angola: Plantation to Penitentiary*. US Army Corps of Engineers, 2007.

Sawyer, Wendy, and Peter Wagner. *Mass Incarceration: The Whole Pie 2024*. Prison Policy Initiative, 2024.

Schafer, Judith Kelleher. *Slavery, the Civil Law, and the Supreme Court of Louisiana*. Louisiana State University Press, 1994.

Schafer, Judith Kelleher. "Slaves and Crime: New Orleans, 1846–1862." In *Local Matters: Race, Crime, and Justice in the Nineteenth-Century South*, edited by Christopher Waldrep and Donald G. Nieman, 53–91. University of Georgia Press, 2001.

Schoeppner, Michael A. *Moral Contagion: Black Atlantic Sailors, Citizenship, and Diplomacy in Antebellum America*. Cambridge University Press, 2019.

Scott, Rebecca J. "Asserting Citizenship and Refusing Stigma: New Orleans Equal-Rights Activists Interpret 1803 and 1848." In *New Orleans, Louisiana and Saint-Louis, Senegal: Mirror Cities in the Atlantic World, 1659–2000s*, edited by Emily Clark, Ibrahima Thioub, and Cécile Vidal, 146–67. Louisiana State University Press, 2019.

Stemen, Don. *The Prison Paradox: More Incarceration Will Not Make Us Safer*. Vera Institute of Justice, 2017.

Stevenson, Bryan. "Why American Prisons Owe Their Cruelty to Slavery." *New York Times Magazine*, August 14, 2019.

Stoddard, Amos. *Sketches, Historical and Descriptive, of Louisiana*. Philadelphia, 1812.

Tansey, Richard. "Out-of-State Free Blacks in Late Antebellum New Orleans." *Louisiana History* 22, no. 4 (1981): 369–86.

Tarter, Michele Lise, and Richard Bell, eds. *Buried Lives: Incarcerated in Early America*. University of Georgia Press, 2012.

Turner, Jennifer. *A Living Death: Life without Parole for Nonviolent Offenses*. American Civil Liberties Union, 2013.

Wacquant, Loïc. "From Slavery to Mass Incarceration: Rethinking the 'Race Question' in the US." *New Left Review* 13 (2002): 41–60.

Wade, Richard C. *Slavery in the Cities: The South, 1820–1860*. Oxford University Press, 1964.

West, Heather C., and William J. Sabol. *Bureau of Justice Statistics Bulletin: Prisoners in 2007*. US Department of Justice, 2008.

Weston, Nathaniel P. "'Frecher Versuch das Arbeitshaus zu zerstören': An Introduction to Vagrancy and Workhouses in New Orleans." *Louisiana History* 41, no. 4 (2000): 467–81.

Widra, Emily. *States of Incarceration: The Global Context 2024*. Prison Policy Initiative, 2024.

Wilson, Samuel, Jr. *The Architecture of Colonial Louisiana: Collected Essays of Samuel Wilson, Jr., F.A.I.A.* Edited by Jean M. Farnsworth and Ann M. Masson. University of Louisiana, 1987.

Wyma, Lee, Katie Wollan, and Ronald B. Reiss. *New Orleans House of Detention*. Federal Emergency Management Agency, 2021.

Zeng, Zhen, and Todd D. Minton. *Census of Jails, 2005–2019—Statistical Tables*. US Department of Justice, 2021.

Acknowledgments

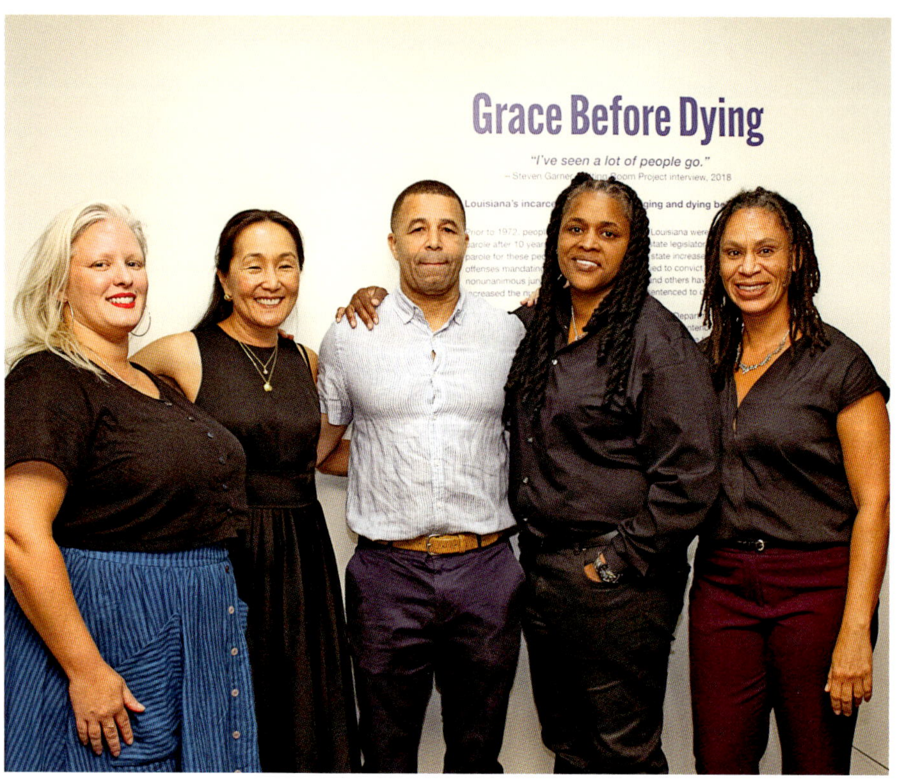

Advisory board members at the *Captive State* opening reception, from left: Katie Hunter-Lowrey, Jee Park, Anthony Hingle Jr., Montrell Carmouche, and Andrea Armstrong. (John Bardes not pictured.)

This publication was made possible with the generous support of the Spark Justice Fund at Borealis Philanthropy. The exhibition *Captive State: Louisiana and the Making of Mass Incarceration* came together thanks to the invaluable contributions of several individuals and organizations. HNOC staff are grateful for the many hours of conversation, tours, and advice from people who have been impacted by incarceration and those whose work touches the history and current operations of the criminal legal system.

The exhibition would not have been possible without the dedicated work of the project's advisory board, whose work on *Captive State* spanned nearly two years: Andrea Armstrong, Loyola University New Orleans College of Law; John Bardes, Louisiana State University; Montrell Carmouche, Operation Restoration; Anthony Hingle Jr., Voice of the Experienced (VOTE) and the Visiting Room Project; Katie Hunter-Lowrey, organizer and survivor of violence; and Jee Park, Innocence Project New Orleans.

HNOC also wishes to thank the Promise of Justice Initiative, Visiting Room Project, Vera Institute of Justice, the family of Shawn Duncan, the family of Cayne Miceli, Sara Gozalo, Curtis Davis, Alvin Reliford, Engrid Hamilton, Beasy Taylor, Derrick Fruga, Steven Garner, Kenneth Woodburn, Theortric Givens, Daryl Waters, Marcus Kondkar, Annie Nisenson, Sophie Cull, Marianne Fisher-Giorlando, Mary Howell, Dominique Dollenmayer, Christian Henrichson, Lee Wyma, Laura Blereau, Sarah Pharaon, Sean Kelley, Lauren Zalut, and Susie Penman.

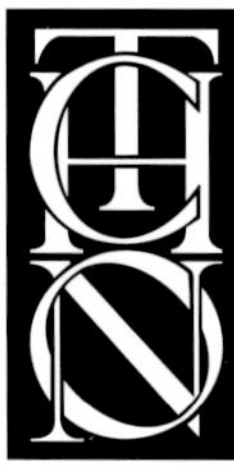

THE HISTORIC NEW ORLEANS COLLECTION

***CAPTIVE STATE* EXHIBITION TEAM**

CURATORS: Eric Seiferth, Kevin T. Harrell, Katherine Jolliff Dunn
EXHIBITION DESIGNER: Cecilia Moscardó
MEDIA PRODUCERS: Xiomara Blanco, Candy Ellison
EXHIBITION COORDINATOR: Matt Farah
CHIEF CURATOR: Jason Wiese
EDITORS: Nick Weldon, Mary M. Garsaud
PREPARATORS: Joe Shores, Robert Gates III, Chris Deris
REGISTRARS: Beth Bahls, Monika M. Cantin
TOUR DEVELOPMENT TEAM: Libby Neidenbach, Joanna Robinson, Douane Waples, Kurt Owens, Jacob Williams, and Craig Fuchs